THE HUNTING FALCON

THE HUNTING FALCON

Bruce A. Haak

ISBN 0-88839-292-3
Copyright © 1992 Bruce A. Haak

Cataloging in Publication Data
Bruce A. Haak
  The hunting falcon

  Includes bibliographical references.
  ISBN 0-88839-292-3 — ISBN 0-88839-302-4 (ltd. ed.)

  1. Falconry. 2. Prairie falcon. I. Title.
  SK321.H23 1992   799.2'32   C92-091559-0

All rights reserved. No part of this publication may be reproduced, stored in a retrieval system or transmitted, in any form or by any means, electronic, mechanical, photocopying, recording, or otherwise, without the prior written permission of Hancock House Publishers.

Printed in Hong Kong

Illustrations: Darryl Barnes and Rick Kline
Front Cover Illustration (Limited Edition): Rick Kline
Front Cover Jacket Photo: Rick Kline
Back Cover Photo: Evelyn Thomas Haak
Production: Lorna Lake

HANCOCK HOUSE PUBLISHERS LTD.
19313 Zero, Avenue, Surrey, B.C. V3S 5J9
(604) 538-1114—538-1557   Fax (604) 538-2262

HANCOCK HOUSE PUBLISHERS
1431 Harrison Avenue, Blaine, WA 98231
(206) 354-6953   Fax (604) 538-2262

Contents

	Dedication	6
	Acknowledgments	6
	Preface	7
1	Introduction	9
2	Fundamentals	49
3	The Prairie Falcon	57
4	Acquiring a Falcon	63
5	Preflight for Falconers	75
6	Training the Eyas	89
7	Passage Prairie Falcon	107
8	Waiting-on Training	121
9	Telemetry	137
10	Falconry Dogs	149
11	Small Game Hawking	157
12	Duck Hawking	171
13	Upland Game Hawking	181
14	Captive Breeding	203
15	Epilogue	217
	Glossary of Terms	230
	Suggested Reading	237

Dedication

For George B. Peden, M.D., falconer, physician, and friend. He wanted to die with his falcon in the air and he got his wish.

Acknowledgments

You never know who your friends are until there is work to be done. For their ideas, constructive criticism, guidance, and encouragement, I extend my heartfelt thanks and appreciation to the following people: Evelyn Thomas Haak for enduring the lost hours, editing, and never losing faith; Rear Admiral Frank S. Haak for being my father and all the right things; Charles H. Schwartz for challenging me to think, write, and improve; Dale Guthormsen for being the prairie falcon's biggest fan; Alva G. Nye, Jr. for a lifetime of good advice; L. Lester Boyd for his good example; William D. MacLeod for editorial comments; Allan R. Cline, Dr. S. Jonathan Denton, and Dr. J. W. (Wes) Pike for showing me the way; to Dennis Mayne who kindly proofread thoroughly at each stage; and to all the people who will never write a book, but make falconry what it is.

Preface

Back within the folds and shrouds of my distant memories there were hawks. I saw them as a small child at the National Zoo in Washington, D.C. Proud captives pierced me with reticent gazes. As the hawks were tethered to their perches, so were they tethered to my destiny. Another day I would return, this time as a gangling youth with a burning curiosity about these hauntingly beautiful birds of prey.

For my entire life, my aunt has lived across the street from the National Zoo. Over the years, her apartment was the base camp from which I launched frequent weekend safaris through this vast zoological exhibit. I trod and retrod the path to the displayed birds of prey many times. Again and again, I was drawn to the crippled peregrine falcon, wing utterly destroyed, that communicated so much through those haughty, coal-black eyes. A chance encounter with a keeper, probably concerned about my catatonic staring, put into motion a chain of events that, in hindsight, was unstoppable. For this kind woman shared with me the name of a most magnanimous gentleman, a local falconer named Alva G. Nye, Jr.

Wise men may argue the function of fate. For me, it was simply the inseparability of conscious desire and unconscious motivation. I was swept away on a current of fascination and excitement about falconry—an activity that I would study and research long before I saw it in practice. Al Nye would direct me, via his student Allan Cline, along the path of knowing and doing. It was a well-counselled tutorial that I would serve under these two men and they must take the credit, or blame, for what I have become.

I believe I am the product of my environment; a course of challenge and study. Small successes and great failures fueled a desire to become competent and, later, to excel at the art of falconry in my own way. While I was traditionally taught, I was never constricted by an arbitrary orthodoxy; I had the freedom to develop. To me, this is the creative link between a student of any discipline and a master.

1 Introduction

This is a practitioner's book on modern falconry in North America. It is dedicated to the small but growing band of men and women who pursue the noble sport in the United States and Canada.

To perceptive readers, modern falconry will appear to be a contradiction in terms. This should not be surprising, for the subject of falconry conjures differing mental images. In our sophisticated, metropolitan, high-tech world of the 1990s, many people picture falconry as an archaic sport once followed by knights and nobles in the chivalrous days of Camelot. Outdoor enthusiasts may instinctively see it as a vestige of a bygone era when hunting was essential for survival. Serious students with a keen sense of its history may recognize that, after forty centuries of evolution, falconry is approaching a pure art form. Inevitably, a few protectionists will be inclined to view falconers as a threat to wild animals or a source of controversy. Those of us who are active falconers share some of these same visions along with others of our own. We see falconry for what it has always been: the practice of hunting wild game with trained birds of prey.

The recorded origins of falconry predate 1200 B.C. to a time when people discovered that hawks, falcons, and eagles—diurnal birds of prey collectively known as raptors—could be trained as useful instruments for providing food. The practice has been perpetuated for more than 4,000 years, and it has survived and adapted to the long sequence of cultural, socioeconomic, and technological changes that have marked the progress of western civilization. What began as a utilitarian approach to putting food on the table assumed a symbolic role in medieval Europe as a favorite sport of the elite nobility. Hunting with falcons gained widespread appeal among the wealthier European classes during the Middle Ages. This is sometimes referred to as the Golden Age of falconry. Yet, we should remember that the Persians, Chinese, Arabs, Indians, and Mongols practiced falconry, often on a grand scale, long before Europeans were introduced to it. The popularity of falconry was destined to decline dramatically with the introduction of gunpowder and the advent of firearms in the fourteenth century. By the late eighteenth century, hunters had turned to more efficient methods for collecting game, but the sport was preserved by a small nucleus of accomplished falconers who valued hunting style and traditions above all else. Those dedicated individuals established the foundations for the western practice of falconry as we know it today. This falconry has subsequently developed into a fine art form in which success is measured by the aesthetics of the flight. Killing game is, therefore, an outcome of high quality flights and not a measure of them. Successful flights are measured by the intangible features of beauty, majesty, and drama they create.

During this century, western falconry has been preserved and maintained chiefly by its loyal followers in the United Kingdom, who successfully sustained the sport between wars. With revived interest after World War II, the British falconry community adapted to meet many significant changes in hunting conditions and restrictive legislation aimed at field sports. Despite those changes, falconry's popularity in the United Kingdom increased substantially during the early 1960s.

In contrast to its status in Britain, falconry in North America has been a recent occurrence. Prior to World War II, serious falconers were a rare breed in the United States, and their activities drew little attention. Only within the past twenty years has falconry achieved limited popularity in North America. Today, about 4,000 falconers practice their ancient art within the confines of modern, urbanized North America.

During the early 1960s, I served my apprenticeship in Virginia under Al Nye and Allan Cline. They guided me with expert advice, strong encouragement, and unlimited patience through the first steps of falconry. After my family moved to the West Coast, I was able to continue my education under the guidance of Dr. Monte Kirven. It was Monte who taught me, via repeated baptisms in San Diego ponds, that falcons could catch ducks. My early mentors opened the doors to a fascinating natural arena long since forgotten by the modern world, and I never turned back. Thanks to their kind efforts, the subsequent three decades of my life have been thoroughly enriched and even dominated by a continuing personal interest in falconry. There is a unique *esprit de corps* among the tight little circle of diehards who take special pride in hunting the old-fashioned way. Obviously, I have many reasons to be grateful to the master falconers who helped me along the way, but I can never repay them directly. So I have written this guide for current and would-be falconers of North America. It is my way of saying thanks to Alva, Allan, Monte, and a host of others.

Falconry is a challenging and rewarding form of hunting that is practiced for different reasons around the world: subsistence hunting, cultural tradition, and recreation. Historically, there have been many interesting types of falconry that employed various hawks, falcons, and eagles to hunt quarry ranging in size from sparrows to deer. This book focuses on a specialized branch of falconry, known as game hawking, which is practiced in North America. For our purposes, game hawking is defined as the hunting of upland game, waterfowl, and other avian quarry with falcons that wait-on or circle high overhead until game is flushed. Game hawking provides the falconer with opportunities to participate vicariously in the dramatic contest between a falcon and its prey. Invariably, the air-to-air duel produces a spectacular display of precision, high-speed aerial pursuit which is the cause of envy among even skilled military aviators. By design, the contestants should be closely matched through the falconer's choice of game, and the outcome of the engagement is a matter of chance. Not surprisingly, the quarry often emerges as the star and victor by escaping the attack. Only through falconry can one witness such dynamic aerial encounters on a regular basis. This privilege is earned by taming and training a wild bird of prey.

Those of us who have experienced the thrill and satisfaction of a successful hunt have learned through trial and error that there are no short cuts to mastering the sport of falconry. The process is lengthy and not without occasional disappointments and frustrations. Traditional methods for training and hunting raptors have long been based on a mix of science, art, and myth, and it is sometimes difficult to tell one from the other. Authoritative sources of information on some of the finer points of game hawking are hard to find. Many important and essential details have been missing from the falconry literature available in the United States and Canada.

The falconers of North America—most of them born since World War II—were educated chiefly by British falconry manuals. A number of fine works have been published in the United Kingdom within the past forty years, and their authors deserve much credit for their contributions. In several important respects, however, these books fall short of meeting the needs of American falconers. By and large, British writers have concentrated on advice for beginners, giving primary emphasis to descriptions of the birds and equipment used in the sport along with instructions for handling and training birds of prey. Almost all of their books devote attention to the familiar peregrine falcon and use peregrine training procedures as the standard for training large falcons. As a rule, the techniques for hunting various species of game have been treated in a cursory manner. While British authors present excellent descriptions of the state of the art in their country, falconry in North America is distinctly different. Britain is a small, densely populated country where the land is largely private and game is considered property of the landowner. Hunting opportunities are limited and expensive. Despite healthy populations of peregrines and other raptors, trapping is prohibited and few are harvested. Most falconry birds are captive-bred or imported.

By comparison, the U.S. is a huge country of varied climates and topography where hunting lands are generally accessible free of charge and game is considered public property. Liberal harvests of native raptors are allowed for falconry purposes with captive breeding supplying certain hard to get species and hybrids. Because many game birds and raptors in North America are unknown in the British Isles, falconers here have experimented with new training techniques and hunting styles. American authors tend to follow the pattern set by their British counterparts. Their books provide guidelines for handling, acquiring, and training birds of prey, but seldom come to grips with the details of catching wild game with them. Since the rudiments of falconry and trapping have been adequately covered by these other authors, I have chosen to concentrate on the application and execution of game hawking techniques.

It came as a severe shock to the U.S. falconry community when the peregrine falcon was listed as an endangered species by the federal government. Because of its wide availability, responsiveness to training, and versatile performance, the peregrine has always been the traditional favorite and almost exclusive hunting partner of many falconers in America and elsewhere. This falcon occupies the most extensive ecological niche of any bird in the world, but it became an inadvertent victim of pesticides and habitat destruction within North America. While the actions of federal and state governments to protect and restore the dwindling peregrine population were encouraged and applauded by the falconry community, those actions had a far-reaching impact on U.S. falconers. For the first time in the long history of the sport, falconers were forced to find suitable alternatives to the familiar peregrine.

My purpose in writing this book is to document recent developments which are ushering in a new era for our sport. Two changes of special interest to North American falconers stem directly from the search for alternatives to peregrines. The challenge to replace this traditional favorite has led to the intensive study of both the prairie falcon and gyrfalcon. Concurrently, substantial research has been directed into the rearing and training of a new class of falcons, often produced by artificial insemination, in captive-breeding programs. These two research efforts have provided a basis for challenging many traditional concepts and suggesting new guidelines for the sport. Another significant but unrelated invention now offers falconers the means to reduce the risk of losing their precious birds through the use of microelectronics. Having participated in each of these efforts, I feel compelled to share some first-hand observations on how these recent developments can be successfully applied in practice.

In this book I have chosen to break with tradition and use the prairie falcon as the example species as opposed to the peregrine. This tack is based on my own experience with training prairie falcons, on the fact that many traditional training techniques for peregrines work poorly with desert falcons and hybrids, and because the prairie falcon represents the only pool of large, wild falcons that can be harvested by North American falconers. While peregrine falcons are comparatively easy to train, prairie falcons are considered by many experienced falconers to be more demanding in terms of skill required. My goal is to provide a framework for training any type of large falcon by using the most challenging species as the example.

As recently as the mid-1960s, the literature provided little information on the nature of the prairie falcon and even less on training them for game hawking. In working with this species as both a falconer and research biologist, I found that many of the falconry community's traditional assumptions concerning prairie falcons were erroneous. We now know that prairie falcons can be trained to be sensational game hawks. They will conform to the falconry regime, but they learn and fly in a manner that is in many ways different from the peregrine. Some practical and proven methods for training prairie falcons and other large falcons are described in later chapters. The philosophy and procedures are based chiefly upon my own experiences, correspondence with other falconers, and extensive observations of trained falcons in the field.

Another key objective of this book is to familiarize falconers with techniques for managing and training imprinted falcons. Because many captive-bred birds are reared entirely by hand, they are psychologically imprinted to people; these birds view the world from a different perspective than a nonimprinted falcon. However, pioneer falconer/hawk breeders like James D. (Jim) Weaver and Lester Boyd have shown, by fine example, that imprinted falcons can become game hawks second to none.

Today, captive breeding supplies rare and unusual falcons that by design or legal necessity are imprinted. Produced on an extremely limited basis only a few years ago, these birds are now available to falconers in North America and elsewhere. Unfortunately, some of the falconers who acquire these birds are perplexed by their behavior, and encounter serious difficulties in training them. Because relatively few falconers are familiar with the techniques for managing imprinted falcons, this new dimension for the sport has met with considerable resistance. The methods for training and handling imprinted falcons differ markedly in both theory and practice from those applicable to passage falcons. Success with one class of bird does not necessarily ensure success with the other. Even some well-known members of falconry's "old guard" have been unable to make the transition smoothly. I am convinced that these problems are the result of insufficient information and faulty theory rather than poorly bred birds or incompetence on the part of the falconers. Based on my own experience, I am also convinced that such problems can be effectively resolved if not completely avoided if the falconer understands the nature of the imprint.

This book is intended as a guide for producing a first class game hawk. It emphasizes practical techniques for training large falcons and providing them with favorable opportunities to hunt wild game birds in North America. These training methods simplify a complex process. They have proven effective in repeated tests by accomplished falconers. Although designed for training large falcons, most of the rearing and handling techniques can be effectively applied to other raptors. I believe this book can provide a falconer with the knowledge essential for success in game hawking, but he or she must gain the necessary field experience to put theory into practice.

Additions to the falconry literature, like many of the technological advances from which falconry has benefitted, should be looked on as contributions toward a falconry continuum. Although it includes some basic information, this book is not intended as a primer. I have not duplicated other works that amply cover the rudimentary details for beginners. As in other fields, there is more than one way to accomplish a falconry goal. Whereas "how to" books generally offer a set of solutions for a problem, I am more concerned with imparting a philosophy that, when combined with practical techniques, yields success. My aim is not to stifle creative thinking about falconry, but to enhance it. The essence of falconry is not the study of an ancient art but the active participation within a dynamic process.

One final note: Falconers are a special breed! Like avid golfers, they regard their sport as not just a game but a way of life. Like purist fly-fishermen, they seek the style and excitement of the activity, not the taking of limits. Like modern bow hunters and black-powder musket shooters, they willingly accept the handicaps of antiquated hunting methods. And, like sailors, they have a special language all their own. Although slightly less salty than the sailor's vocabulary, many of the falconer's terms can be just as cryptic to the uninitiated. For this reason, I have appended a glossary for the benefit of those readers new to falconry.

Immature prairie falcon with Hungarian partridge. *Photo: Rick Kline*

Red-naped shaheen. *Photo: Ed Levine*

Opposite page: Peale's peregrine. *Photo: Author*

Rocky Mountain peregrine falcon. *Photo: Rick Kline*

Eyass female prairie falcon.

Photos: Author

Opposite page: Gyr/peregrine female.

Gyr/peregrine female.

A typical prairie falcon eyrie in central Oregon. Falcons often occupy prominent landmarks affording broad vistas.
Photo: Author

Haggard Peale's peregrine at her eyrie, Queen Charlotte Islands, British Columbia.
Photo: David Hancock

Author rappelling to falcon eyrie. Note backpack for transporting eyasses to the ground safely. *Photo: William Grummer*

A productive prairie falcon eyrie is often crowded with young. This cavity held five eyasses.

Photos: Author

Eyas prairie falcons taken at this stage, approximately four-weeks old, require extra care to overcome their fear of handling.

Opposite page: Chris Merker with a small downy prairie falcon. This eyas is an ideal age for imprinting.

Eyas peregrine tiercel and falcon being dual socialized. These falcons will be as well-adjusted as imprints but will mate with other falcons when mature.

It is never too early to hood train an eyas. These two peregrines are hooded before being fed.

Photos: Author

Eyasses, like this imprinted prairie falcon, love to bathe.

A perky eyas prairie falcon may fledge without warning. If equipped with a transmitter, eyasses may be recovered quickly from their initial exploratory flights.

Photos: Author

Cast of eyas peregrines at tame hack.

Imprints, like this gyrfalcon, enjoy playing with toys.

Tame hacking gives eyasses a chance to build condition and explore their surroundings. →

Photos: Author

The endearing nature of imprints allows for a close relationship. →

Imprinted prairie falcon sleeping on the job.

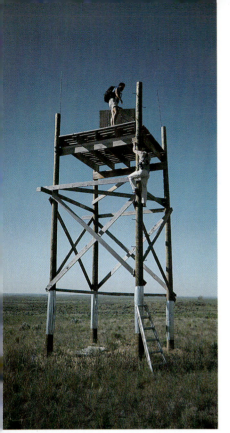

Hack tower with mammalian predator guards on poles. *Photo: Author*

Hack tower—Bahrain. *Photo: Charles H. Schwartz*

Cohort-reared eyasses are easy to train and make excellent breeding stock. *Photo: Author*

Author's daughter with her falcon. *Photo: Author*

Mike Yates removes a passage tundra peregrine from a pigeon harness.

Photos: Author

Falcons must be quickly and carefully removed from nets to prevent feather damage. →

A defiant haggard prairie tiercel trapped with a dho-gazza.

A haggard prairie tiercel trapped during winter. All haggards must be released immediately.

A fine passage prairie tiercel.

Photos: Author

A productive morning of trapping.

An eyas prairie falcon trapped at an eyrie two to three weeks after fledging is essentially a hacked eyas. →

Radio transmitter used for locating lost falcons. *Photo: Author*

Hooded gyrfalcon with tail-mounted transmitter. *Photo: Ronald G. Clarke*

Antenna quiver and receiver pack for carrying telemetry. *Photo: Ed Levine*

Opposite page: Charles Schwartz with a freshly trapped prairie falcon. *Photo: Author*

Receiver and antenna combination carried by a sling. *Photo: Author*

The partridge hawking team. Author with English pointer and intermewed red-naped shaheen.

Photo: Steve Van Zandt

Cock pheasants are difficult to flush at the right time.

Photo: Author

Intermewed passage red-naped shaheen and a gray partridge; a perfect match.

Photo: Author

Opposite page: Passage prairie falcon with quail.

Photo: Rick Kline

Hybrid prairie/peregrine falcon with a sage grouse.

Photo: Autho.

Eyas prairie falcon with cock pheasant. Pheasants can be difficult quarry to subdue on the ground.
Photo: Author

Intermewed passage prairie falcon with gray partridge on the fist.

Photo: Randy Carnahan

Alaska gerkin with a willow ptarmigan.
Photo: Ronald G. Clarke

Intermewed eyas prairie falcon with a sharp-tailed grouse.   *Photo: Dale Guthormsen*

A white gyr/peregrine hybrid and an English pointer make a handsome team for sage grouse.
↓   *Photo: Charles H. Schwartz*

Intermewed eyas Peale's peregrine and a midwinter sage grouse.

Photos: Charles H. Schwartz

An aggressive imprinted Peale's peregrine falcon takes a sage grouse.

Intermewed passage prairie falcon puts a gadwall on ice.

Photos: Author

Intermewed passage prairie falcon with a green-winged teal. Ducks of all sizes make excellent quarry for falcons.

Passage gyrfalcon captures a mallard.   *Photo: Rick Kline*

Midwinter duck hawking can be challenging sport. Here, an intermewed passage red-naped shaheen captures a drake mallard.   *Photo: Author*

There are days when things just go right. *Photo: Author*

Opposite page: Anatum peregrine with a green-winged teal. *Photo: Rick Kline*

Steve Bilbro's breeding chamber built after the design by Les Boyd.

Photos: Author

A "natural" pair of Peale's peregrines bred by Dave Jamieson.

Imprinted Barbary falcon with a clutch of eggs. *Photo: Charles H. Schwartz*

Peale's peregrine, bred by David Hancock, incubating her eggs. *Photo: David Hancock*

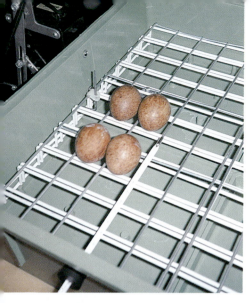

↑ Newly hatched peregrine chick arrives wet and exhausted.
Photo: Author

↑ ← The temperature and humidity of the incubator are carefully controlled so that the falcon eggs will hatch. *Photo: Author*

← Author feeding day-old peregrine chick.
Photo: Evelyn Thomas Haak

↓ Young falcons eat about every three hours between dawn and dusk. *Photo: Bruce Stoddard*

Falcons raised in groups or "cohorts" help keep each other warm and active.

← Young falcons require warmth until they are about ten days of age.

At about ten days of age, eyasses can begin feeding themselves well-ground meat.   *Photos: Author*

A first-year gyrfalcon shows that maternal instincts are deep-seated in birds of prey. *Photo: Author*

Adult falcons that feed and care for young will save the breeder countless hours of toil. *Photo: Paula S. Becker*

2 Fundamentals

Aldo Leopold, the noted naturalist, once called falconry the "perfect hobby." Undoubtedly, he was referring to the fact that a falconer is required to become well-informed in a broad range of technical subjects and proficient in performing a diversity of practical tasks. The sport combines wildlife study, outdoor recreation, mental challenge, emotional stimulation, and physical exercise. It is a personal and often solitary sport for individuals willing to accept the demands of a "do-it-yourself" hobby. Falconry is a series of lessons in problem solving. Mastery depends in large degree upon the falconer's knowledge, skill, experience, powers of observation, and ability to learn.

Falconry has many facets. Those of us who pursue falconry have frequently faced new and perplexing situations for which we could find no textbook solutions. So we learned the hard way. With the aid of that 20/20 hindsight, I believe that a discussion of a few fundamentals will contribute to a better understanding of falconry's multiple dimensions.

In simple terms, game hawking is an outdoor sport in which the falconer, a hunting dog, and a trained falcon perform as a coordinated team in pursuit of quarry. The falconer is the team leader, strategic planner, and tactician. The dog assists the falconer in locating, marking, and flushing game. Both the falconer and the dog play essential parts in game hawking. In the final analysis, however, the team's performance in the field is ultimately measured by the falcon. The hunting falcon's role is essentially identical to its role as a wild bird of prey.

As one of nature's superbly designed winged creatures, the falcon is endowed with excellent aerodynamic characteristics, extraordinary visual acuity, and an aggressive hunting style. This unique combination of capabilities enables the falcon to spot prey at long distances and use its sensational flying powers to attack game birds in midair. The feathered hunter is ideally equipped for a form of air-to-air pursuit which occurs routinely in the wild. In nature's scheme of things, all birds of prey attack, kill, and eat a variety of birds and small mammals in order to survive. Although squeamish individuals may prefer to pretend otherwise, these necessary actions occur as a common, daily phenomenon—whether or not observed by humans. Such combat is always governed by the laws of nature; the odds are seldom stacked in the raptor's favor. A wild falcon must frequently attempt three or more attacks before achieving a kill, but the results of each trial tend to be hit or miss in character. If the falcon fails to score, the prey escapes.

The falcon's behavior is constantly affected by its food, its physical condition, the weather, its relationship with the falconer, and the actions of the game bird it is hunting. Removed from its natural habitat, the beautiful bird of prey will become dependent upon its human partner. For this reason, the falconer must have the time, temperament, and strong sense of moral obligation to provide for the bird's proper care and feeding on a daily, long-term basis. One must first tame the wild raptor, develop a close rapport, and establish a mutual trust and confidence. Once this bond is cemented, the bird is ready to be trained as a hunting partner. How this is done can be described succinctly: slowly and carefully!

From the outset, the would-be falconer should clearly understand that the sport is regulated by federal and state governments and also by the falconers themselves. Current regulations establish strict guidelines for testing and licensing falconers, and prescribe mandatory minimum standards for facilities in which birds of prey are held. Government agencies regulate the

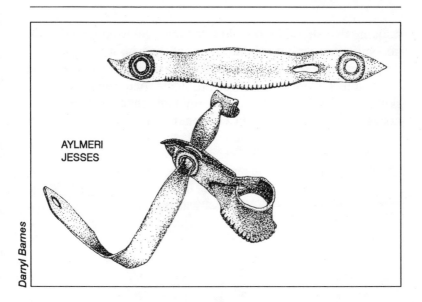

AYLMERI JESSES

Darryl Barnes

seasons and harvests of both the raptors used in falconry and the game species hunted in the sport. All birds of prey are strictly protected by law.

U.S. federal and state regulations group falconers into three separate classes according to their experience in the sport. The beginner or "novice" is required to be an apprentice to a more experienced tutor during the initial phase of training. One must pass an examination on falconry and possess adequate facilities and equipment for the care of a bird.

As an apprentice, the beginner acquires the rudimentary skills to handle and care for a wild bird of prey and provide it with fresh food. Although much of the equipment needed for handling birds of prey is readily available from commercial sources, the novice is encouraged to learn to make most of what he or she will need. This includes hoods, gauntlets, leashes, jesses, perches, mews, pigeon lofts, and other needed facilities. In addition, the novice must master the language of falconry, study the natural history of birds of prey and the game species to be hunted, and become familiar with the diseases and maladies which can afflict birds of prey. This is akin to requiring a budding fly-fisherman to build a rod and reel from scratch and become a competent fish biologist before even wetting a line! The apprenticeship gives the beginning falconer important insights into falconry's logistical problems. Acquiring the basic skills presents the novice with a formidable challenge: these are necessary steps in becoming a falconer.

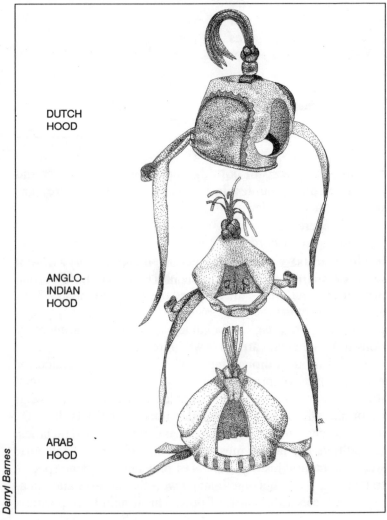

Following the apprenticeship, the falconer can start to concentrate on the technical aspects of game hawking. By this time, the beginner will have become adept at handling and training a raptor, and is ready to take on more demanding tasks. The next objective is to acquire the requisite skills for hunting a variety of wild game with different species of hawks and falcons. The falconer must learn to plan the hunt, handle the dog, locate game, and execute strategies that present the raptor with the best prospects for successful performance in the field. Because the raptor often requires many chances to catch game, the falconer must become proficient at supplying the bird with advantageous hunting opportunities. A major part of the falconer's efforts is directed toward manipulating the hunting situation in favor of the hawk or falcon.

Eventually, the falconer will have some latitude in choosing a raptor. At this point, there is an important issue to be resolved by realistic thinking and common sense. *Before* making a choice, one needs to take stock of the game hawking opportunities and determine what game species are available, then strive for a good match between the raptor and the likely quarry. Otherwise, one may acquire a bird totally unsuited to the hunting situation. The falconer cannot expect a tiercel prairie falcon to tackle a burly sage grouse, nor can one expect to tally a decent score on sparrows with a gyrfalcon. There may be a certain amount of ego gratification in possessing one of the large, exotic falcons, but its role as a practical hunting partner can be quite limited. The falconer's choice between a hawk or falcon should always be based upon the game available, local cover and lay of the land. Although hawks and falcons fly and hunt in different ways, both perform well as game hawks when matched against appropriate quarry.

Most falconers prefer to use hawks for hunting because large falcons are difficult to train and require open space. While space requirements for large falcons vary for different quarry, one needs an uninterrupted view of the flight for approximately one mile in all directions. Hawks attack game by flying it down in the air or chasing it into cover before grabbing or "binding" to it. The species commonly used include the red-tailed hawk, goshawk, Cooper's hawk, and Harris hawk. These birds are effective in mixed woodlot and field situations that would be unsuitable for hunting falcons. An opportunist by nature, the hawk is often carried on the falconer's gloved hand and released when game is flushed to pursue it straightaway. This is done in much the same way as a shooter would stalk game. The falconer takes opportunities that arise while working through the fields or following the lead of a hunting dog. This form of hunting lends itself well to the pursuit of rabbits and upland-game birds such as quail and pheasants.

Large falcons, such as prairie falcons and peregrine falcons, comprise a group of specialized birds which pursue their quarry in high-speed aerial attacks. In a maneuver which resembles precision dive bombing, these birds first achieve an altitude advantage over their quarry, then convert that advantage to speed in a steep descent called a stoop. With terminal speeds which may approach 200 miles per hour, their diving attacks often prevent them from slowing enough to grab their prey. Instead, they strike with a karate-style blow that sends their prey tumbling through the air. It is the lightning-fast attack and the decisive strike of a stooping falcon, more than anything else, which has endeared the sport to falconers throughout the centuries and kindled their respect for this elegant bird of prey. Falcons are flown in open country where their flying style can be used to greatest advantage and where the falconer can keep track of the flight.

Falcons undergo sophisticated and time-consuming training for a tactic known as waiting-on. They learn to leave the falconer's fist and circle hundreds of feet overhead while waiting for game to be flushed or served. The falconer must produce game within a reasonable amount of time; this varies with the age, experience, and personality of the falcon. Otherwise, the bird is likely to fly away or land in confusion. It is the falcon's confidence in the falconer's ability to supply game that prevents it from leaving. To ensure this confidence, falcons are often flown at marked game that has been located prior to the release of the falcon. With upland game, the falconer tries to spot birds feeding in the open, or relies on a pointing dog. Steady pointers are essential for this type of hawking, and falconers must teach their dogs to work as a team with the bird. Waterfowl provide an interesting alternative and are the mainstay for many who hunt with falcons. Ducks can often be located on small ponds, and the falcon can be released to wait-on while the falconer gets close enough to flush them.

Style has always been the essence of falconry. It is the drama and spectacle of the chase that motivates falconers to pursue their art with such fervor.

Special seasons coupled with reduced bag limits, allow falconers to pursue their sport for up to seven months per year. This has not led to a sharp increase in the number of participants. Furthermore, recent government findings confirm that falconry has had no measurable impact on game or raptor populations due to the difficult nature of the sport.

In the United States, shooting seasons don't provide ample opportunities to train raptors and bring them into hunting condition. For this reason, almost all states have adopted special falconry seasons that begin early in the year, in advance of regular shooting seasons. Falconers are able to challenge their hawks with hunting situations that increase in difficulty as the season progresses. It is extremely difficult to train young hawks and falcons on wise, old game birds; early seasons give young raptors a chance to practice their hunting skills on young, inexperienced quarry just as they would in the wild. Wild birds of prey must hunt daily for food. During the hunting season, raptors must be exercised on most days in order to maintain the physical stamina and technical skills to outfly and strike down their prey. As a rule, falconry seasons continue through the regular gun hunting seasons. Because hawking is not likely to put undue pressure on game populations, some states have authorized extended falconry seasons for upland game, waterfowl, and rabbits.

Falconers cannot compete with shotgunners. The average gunner can get much more action in a small amount of time without the responsibility of caring for a trained raptor for 365 days a year. Competition for game is never a serious concern to falconers, but competition for hunting areas is an entirely different matter. During the shooting season, falconers must always take special precautions to safeguard their trained raptors. All birds of prey are strictly protected by law, but this law is broken all too often! The unfortunate fact is that trained birds of prey, and many wild ones, continue to be shot. Malicious individuals or those ignorant of the important role which raptors play in nature cause falconers to seek safe places to fly their birds. In this regard, extended falconry seasons are a welcome privilege. Extended seasons allow falconers to spend time looking for game instead of looking out for trouble.

The road to becoming a master falconer is a long one. It requires years of training, lots of energy, and considerable know-how to bring a falcon into hunting condition. The ultimate rewards come from the drama of the well-planned hunt in which the trained falcon is ideally matched to its quarry. One will never see a flock of ducks wheel with such skill around the edge of a pond as when a prairie falcon is waiting-on, blanketing their every move. Nor will one ever observe a more exciting demonstration of aerial acrobatics than when a mourning dove displays its repertoire of midair stalls and high-speed reversals to evade a stooping falcon. Such artful exhibitions are equaled or surpassed only by the beautiful flight of the hunting falcon executing the role for which it has been trained. It is the quality of the flight and the mastery of worthy opponents which give the falconer the greatest reward.

Falconry is truly one of the outdoor sports where the premium is placed on style, aesthetic appreciation, and the quality of the recreational experience. It is the skill and challenge that count, rather than the number of game birds taken. However, falcons need a number of successful flights to develop persistence on game and a reasonable acceptance of defeat. Style and success go in unison. This is what falconry is all about!

3 The Prairie Falcon

Traditional falconers pursued their art in a manner that emphasized the sporting character of game hawking. Long before governments regulated them, falconers devised precepts and conventions to be observed in the practice of falconry. The laws of practicality were employed to match the falcon and its quarry—a central theme throughout much of the falconry literature and still a dominant factor in the selection of a game hawk.

In recent years, the availability of falcons through captive breeding, the application of new training techniques and equipment, and the fervent pursuit of extremely challenging quarry have stimulated a considerable amount of experimentation in North America. In some cases, ground-breaking successes have been achieved. There are now falcons that routinely wait-on thousands of feet above the falconer when hunting, and extremely difficult quarry is being captured regularly by trained falcons. There have also been failures, particularly when a falcon and quarry have been mismatched, that resulted in the death of the falcon. The net result, however, is that the horizons of falconry have been expanded, the concept of "feasible" redefined. Perched prominently on the cutting edge of much of this experimentation has been the prairie falcon.

In theory, the process of choosing a hawk can be viewed as a sequence of logical steps. One first decides what game species to hunt, and which of the raptors are possible candidates. Next, the candidates are ranked according to their suitability for the intended quarry. For practical purposes, the raptor must be large enough to deal efficiently with its prey. Ideally, the game hawk candidate will be an aggressive and physically tough hunter with sufficient weight, speed, and determination to strike a lethal blow in the stoop or subdue the game to which it has bound. After listing the promising candidates, the falconer can then evaluate each in terms of its current availability and responsiveness to training. In this manner, a hunting partner can be acquired, trained, and matched against game birds in the field.

In practice, the task of choosing a game hawk is far less complicated than the foregoing description may suggest. The one all-important prerequisite for success in modifying a raptor's behavior for falconry purposes is to first find out what makes the species "tick." As K. and M. Breland have noted, "the behavior of any species cannot be adequately understood, predicted or controlled without knowledge of its instinctive patterns, evolutionary history and ecological niche."

The North American falconer has many interesting choices of winged quarry, depending on where the falconer lives. Populations of pheasant, partridge, quail, prairie grouse, and other game species are distributed with varying densities across the United States and Canada. Migratory waterfowl offer other attractive possibilities. After determining which game bird can be hunted with regularity, the falconer then has a sound basis for selecting a raptor. In view of their relatively wide range, pheasants and ducks will probably be high on the list of intended quarry. If so, the choice of a game hawk will be limited to the larger species.

Prior to the 1970s, the selection of a falcon for hunting North American game birds was a simple, straightforward process. The peregrine falcon has always been the obvious answer to the falconer's needs, and there were few reasons to consider other alternatives. Most falconers found peregrines to be the easiest large falcon to acquire. Much detailed information was available concerning their behavior and excellent hunting characteristics. Their sporting nature, ease of training, reliability in the field, and willingness to pursue a number of quarries made peregrines the classic favorite of falconers in North America, Britain, and elsewhere. Unfortunately, this all changed abruptly in 1973 with the passage of the Endangered Species Act. When the peregrine was declared off limits, U.S. falconers were forced to search for a new hunting partner. To the surprise of many, they didn't have to look far.

Prairie falcons are native to western North America, and substantial populations have been reported in many regions west of the Mississippi River since the 1940s. However, these birds remained an enigma for many years and the available literature provided few insights into the nature of the species. When peregrines were easy to get, prairie falcons were largely ignored by North American falconers, specifically those in the eastern half of the continent. Little in the way of falconry literature addressed either their training or performance in the field before the mid-1960s. Only a few pioneering individuals, such as Morlan Nelson of Boise, Idaho, had recognized and exploited the prairie falcon's potential as a hunting partner. It is curious to note, however, that during this time certain European falconers regarded them highly for flights out of the hood at rooks and crows.

The prairie falcon is an intermediate-sized falcon similar in weight to the arctic peregrine. Like the peregrine, the prairie falcon is versatile and extremely well-suited to the hunting conditions frequently encountered in restricted suburban environments. The female prairie falcon is an excellent match for upland game birds and waterfowl, including big ducks and cock pheasants. Her aggressive nature and determination allow the prairie falcon to deal efficiently with game, and she will attack and pursue her quarry with surprising fervor. Some female prairie falcons have downed birds as large as geese and sage grouse, although most falcons have the good sense to avoid a mismatch with such outsized game.

In terms of its flying qualities, the prairie falcon ranks among the best of the game hawk candidates. It combines excellent speed and maneuverability by virtue of its aerodynamic shape and conformation. Attack effectiveness depends more on the falcon's pitch, positioning and ability to modify its diving approach and smoothly cut the corners to intercept its prey. The fairly light wing loading (weight versus wing area) of the prairie falcon enables it to correct its flight path easily and change direction rapidly during the course of a stoop. The falcon is thus able to compensate quickly for the evasive actions of its prey. This ability is even more pronounced in the tiercels. With even lighter wing loadings than the females, the males have an adroitness that permits them to capture some of the more evasive small game species.

The prairie falcon evolved in a harsh desert environment that required the bird to become extremely adaptable and versatile in order to survive. The need to pursue both avian and mammalian prey species predisposed the falcon to employ a variety of strategies for successfully exploiting any hunting opportunity. Like other wild raptors, the prairie falcon uses multiple attack styles while foraging for food. Consistent with the nature of its environment, this falcon is particularly adept at flying down elusive birds across open plains. Having learned the difference between eating and starving in a sparse desert habitat, the prairie falcon will characteristically continue in relentless, hot pursuit of evasive game, often crashing through cover that the average peregrine would not attempt to enter.

The aggressive nature of this species is apparent in the reckless abandon with which many prairie falcons strike game. This falcon attempts to strike with a force that kills or seriously debilitates game in the air, leaving the quarry with little ability to fight off the falcon on the ground. The proportionately longer legs of the prairie falcon, as compared with the peregrine, are believed to enhance this striking ability, and the propensity to hit prey very hard is a well-documented trait of the species. This is an admirable trait in a game hawk for most situations, but a special word of caution is in order. The falconer should be keenly aware that the prairie falcon's aggressive hunting style can actually cause a serious problem. If the falcon is improperly matched against an excessively large game bird, it may strike the quarry with enough force to injure itself. Unfortunately, I know of numerous instances in which prairie falcons have been injured or killed in this manner.

In some ways, the prairie falcon is equivalent to the peregrine for game hawking in North America. The two species are similar in size, speed, and hunting versatility. Hunting situations normally encountered by the majority of falconers will present the prairie falcon with opportunities to use its attributes to greatest advantage. When a pheasant or duck is flushed directly underneath it, the prairie falcon will attack and strike the quarry just as would a wild raptor foraging over the plains. The same energy and aggression that would otherwise be expended in numerous attempts to make a kill in the wild will be directed into one blistering stoop and knockdown blow. In the field, the prairie falcon leaves no doubt that it can hold its own against the peregrine as a stylish and dedicated hunting companion.

In some segments of the falconry community, there has been widespread misinformation that waiting-on is an unnatural form of hunting for the prairie falcon. Nothing could be further from the truth. I have been observing wild prairie falcons for over twenty years, and I have frequently seen them stoop from tremendous heights in attempts to make a kill. On one outing, I watched a female ringing-up to almost 1,000 feet and stooping repeatedly in dramatic style for well over thirty minutes.

In fact, a large part of a wild prairie falcon's day may be spent soaring, in readiness to stoop into action at some unsuspecting prey. This is not to say that prairie falcons do not hunt regularly from power poles and low perches, but it is important to note that the high stoop is part of their natural repertoire. This particular hunting technique enhances the falcon's ability to detect quarry and achieve the speed needed to overhaul swift-flying birds. Field studies have confirmed that the high stoop is one of several basic attack styles exhibited by all large falcons when foraging, and is one of six specific methods typical of the wild prairie falcon.

We know that prairie falcons learn, fly, and hunt in ways that differ from the peregrine, but they will nevertheless perform with equal effectiveness in the role of the classic hunting falcon. Like any raptor species, the prairie falcon learns the catechism of the game hawk through repetition. The bird's training is accomplished in a self-reinforcing sequence of confidence-building exercises; and the more it succeeds, the harder it will try. A well-schooled prairie falcon knows that positioning is everything, and will gain its place above the falconer in anticipation of the chance to demonstrate its skills. Once committed to its role as a hunting partner, the falcon becomes more trustworthy, thus allowing the falconer to place the bird in increasingly challenging situations. The quest to take a good falcon and make it better, to find its limits and tax them appropriately, is what the sport of falconry is all about. Without question, the trained prairie falcon will respond willingly to such challenges and reward the falconer with style, courage, and convincing performance.

There is probably some truth to that old adage: "The more things change, the more they remain the same." For the majority of North American falconers, selection of a game hawk continues to be a simple and straightforward process. The objective remains the same: to choose a raptor that can be readily acquired, effectively trained, and properly matched against game birds in the field. Since the options for wild birds are constrained by law, however, the result is now different from the standard answer of earlier decades. In effect, the "old standby" peregrine has undergone a sort of role reversal with the previously "unknown" prairie falcon, and now the prairie falcon is the only viable candidate currently available from the wild as a large hunting falcon. Fortunately for the North American falconry community, the prairie falcon is truly an outstanding game hawk capable of upholding the best traditions of the sport.

4 Acquiring a Falcon

Henry and John were the best of friends. The pioneer spirit was alive and well in Henry, a retired logger who had spent most of his life in remote lumber camps. In the early days, without the benefit of formal guidance, he had taught himself falconry. Here was an old-fashioned, do-it-yourself woodsman, determined to do things his way. When Henry wanted a goshawk to train, he combed the woods, found a nest with several branchers sitting in a tall conifer, and expertly shot the limb out from under one of them—not exactly your textbook method for collecting an eyas shortwing! John, on the other hand, was of a younger generation with a wider exposure to falconry. A tough, young state trooper and family man, John found a lot of common ground with the elder Henry. Living in a small western town and sharing interests in falconry and the out-of-doors, they spent much time together.

When it came to searching out prairie falcon eyries, these men were always close-lipped about where they went and what they found. This was in keeping with the falconry tradition of protecting nest locations from disturbance and forcing would-be falconers to pay their dues by finding their own eyries. However, they extended this concept to the extreme and didn't even tell family members which direction they were going.

In their part of the high desert, the best time for taking eyas prairie falcons was during the first week of June. On a "bluebird" clear summer morning, Henry and John packed their gear and drove to the rugged canyon country. Far from people and civilization was a "secret" eyrie. From previous reconnaissance trips, the men knew that this eyrie held numerous eyasses, and it was time to collect two of them for training.

I don't know how much formal training or experience John had in rappelling and rock-climbing techniques. But somewhere in the process of making his way down the face of the cliff, John lost control of the rope and fell to the earth below. The fall injured John's back. Henry, in a state of utter panic, was making his way back to the car to go for help when he suffered a heart attack and died. For three days, Search and Rescue operations scoured the desert mountains searching for the men. All their friends and area falconers were contacted in an attempt to narrow the investigation area. Finally, after exploring vague leads and hunches, the authorities found them. Delirious and in excruciating pain, John had dragged himself in the wrong direction, away from the road.

This grim tale sends many messages. The first is that just about every facet of falconry demands preparation. Our zeal for the sport should never outweigh the logical dictates of personal safety. After all, falconry is supposed to be fun. Staring death in the face from several hundred feet above a rocky talus slope cannot be categorized as a recreational experience. Another thing to keep in mind is that eyasses taken from short, easily accessible cliffs are just as good as those taken from high, crumbling cliffs.

Any man or woman who pursues falconry must quickly come to grips with some self-evident facts. The first of these is that life, liberty, and the pursuit of happiness as a falconer do not begin until one possesses one's own game hawk. The second is that all falconers are definitely not created equal. All are unique individuals with distinctly different talents, experiences, resources, and life styles. Each one has compelling, practical reasons to choose a hawk to fit his or her personal circumstances. In effect, matching the falcon to the falconer becomes just as important as matching it to the intended quarry.

Before selecting a game hawk, every falconer should be keenly aware that the age and upbringing of the raptor will largely determine the methods and time schedules for bringing the bird into hunting condition. In most cases, there will be several alternatives from which to choose. Two of these are the fully developed, wild "passage" falcon and the "eyas." (In the parlance of falconry, an "eyas" is any bird taken before it can fly.) Depending on its age, the eyas may become psychologically imprinted, thus introducing additional choices. Alternative sources are also beginning to command increased attention. Historically, the chief concern of North American falconers was the taking of passage or eyas birds from the wild. Now, captive breeding provides a significant number of birds for falconry. Before making a final selection, the prudent falconer will need to explore the pros and cons of passage falcons versus eyasses, imprinted versus nonimprinted eyasses, and wild-taken versus captive-bred birds as game-hawk candidates.

A falcon's age is one of the most important factors affecting its responsiveness to training. As with other creatures, the bird's psyche is extremely complex, and its behavioral development is closely linked to its physical and mental growth. Behavioral studies have confirmed similar linkages in a variety of birds and mammals, and age was found to have a consistently strong influence on training responses. Controlled experiments with selected species have shown that there is some optimum age at which their training should commence. Undoubtedly, there is an optimum age at which a falcon should begin its training, but the limited data now available do not permit accurate estimates. Few falconers could ever expect to have either the luck or luxury of finding birds of exactly the right age. Consequently, we must learn to deal effectively with raptors of all ages. A good falconer can build a fine rapport with almost any kind of falcon.

66 Acquiring a Falcon

One of the options available to many falconers is to take a passage prairie falcon from the wild. Passage falcons do not require all the tedious preliminaries and graduated lessons necessary for training and hunting an eyas. Consequently, they may be a practical choice for the falconer whose spare time is limited. Most passage falcons are trapped between September and January. They are already fully-conditioned, experienced hunters when they are taken, and are easily entered to the preferred game species. The latter attribute can be extremely helpful under certain conditions, particularly when the falconer may have less hunting experience than the passage falcon. The passager may also be an excellent candidate for game hawking in areas where quality flights are at a premium—where upland game are scarce or migratory waterfowl are only seasonally abundant.

It would be unusual to find a passage prairie falcon that was not an accomplished and aggressive hunter. The falcon will no doubt be ready and willing to chase game flushed properly beneath it. On the other hand, the falconer must be ready and willing to accept the substantial risks along with the rewards of hunting a passage falcon. One must be able to ensure opportunities for the falcon to kill on a regular basis, and cannot allow the fresh passager much latitude in the field. Only in this manner can one build the necessary strong bond of trust and confidence with the bird and keep the wayward passager from going its separate way. Lacking that special bond, the bird may be tempted to take a perch rather than fly or—worse—it may decide to leave the falconer in search of prey elsewhere. A passage falcon will become a steady and reliable hunting partner over a period of several seasons, but the bird is best regarded as a faithless love that may decide to go "over the hill."

As an alternative to the risky passager, the eyas presents the falconer with the opportunity to acquire and train a hunting partner for reliable performance in the field. Eyasses are currently classified according to their origin, age, and mental state. Whether an eyas is taken from the wild or captive bred has little bearing on the training methods to be used. However, birds taken at different ages usually will require different approaches.

As a rule, eyasses taken before twenty-one days of age become psychologically imprinted, and may eventually respond sexually to their trainer and pair-bond (court and mate) with him or her. Due to their early acclimation, the imprints tend to be easier to handle than older eyasses, and they are very dependable in the field. Imprints often return to the falconer when other falcons might not. They also appear to adapt more readily to the captive environment. However, some imprinted females become aggressive and attack other people when they mature. Initially, these birds are extremely fragile and they require special care and brooding before gaining their feathers. Given the choice, I would take an eyas at the age when the tail feathers are between one-quarter and one inch in length.

The older, nonimprinted eyas tends to progress more slowly in the training schedule. At first, the older eyas is likely to display fear and anxiety, and the falconer must handle the bird's initial apprehensions carefully.

Nevertheless, it is not necessarily true that training difficulty increases in proportion to the age at which the eyas is taken. Based on his extensive experience with raising numerous eyas prairie falcons of all ages, Dale Guthormsen of Saskatchewan, Canada, considers the 5- to 6-week-old eyas much easier to handle than the 3- to 4-week-old birds.

Understanding the complex psyche of a falcon is the key to success in falconry, and is also important in captive-breeding programs. Currently, it is believed that the close association with a human in a falconry relationship does much to predispose both imprinted and nonimprinted falcons toward future breeding. Because of their very early association with people, it is not unusual for imprints to respond sexually to their trainers. On the other hand, some older eyasses and even a few passage falcons have also been known to pair-bond with falconers or breeders. Under certain conditions, such responses may result in an egg-laying female or a semen-donating male. The birds may then be mated through artificial insemination to produce more stock for falconry or breeding projects. Although their training and breeding are both labor-intensive tasks, these birds are proving to be a valuable source of falcons.

Captive-bred falcons reared by their parents, or cohorts of young falcons raised together in isolation, again develop into promising breeding stock, particularly after being flown and handled for a season or two. With the greater availability of these birds through captive propagation, as well as the relative ease with which they may be trained, such birds have become highly regarded by the falconry community.

Given the alternatives above, the falconers of North America should have little difficulty in choosing a game hawk to match their personal circumstances. Some falconers will consider passage falcons to be acceptable risks, and they can employ any number of time-tested trapping methods to acquire their birds. In the near term, at least, many falconers have gravitated to captive-bred falcons because they are available and affordable. In western North America, a number of falconers still opt for the wild eyas due to their ready availability.

Let us first consider the falconer who chooses to take an eyas prairie falcon as his or her game hawk. Even though the weather in May and June, the eyas-taking season, is generally pleasant, this is by no means a trivial excursion into the outdoors. The falconer will need to know how to locate the eyrie and how to climb into it safely. In effect, the falconer is making a decision to climb some remote cliff, take a wild eyas from its nest, and get back home without getting injured or harming the falcon. As it turns out, rock climbing happens to be one of the key ingredients in Aldo Leopold's concept of the "perfect hobby." As I suggested earlier, falconry is many things, sometimes even downright dangerous!

Prairie falcons nest on cliffs in remote country. They habitually seek high places that offer a grand vista of the surrounding countryside and access to wind currents or thermals. The birds will use whatever cliffs are available, and there is no particular height criterion for a prairie falcon eyrie. Likely nesting structures may range from rock piles with heights of only fifteen feet to huge escarpments that garland high, forested peaks. Nor is there any set of directional orientation for prairie falcon eyries. I have found them facing all points of the compass. Productive areas to search include rimrock cliffs, buttes, and outcroppings adjacent to open range, desert, or agricultural land. A nest will often be hidden within a prominent landmark in a basin or valley.

The search for the eyrie can prove both time-consuming and physically taxing. The falconer will always benefit from thorough planning, and should examine available topographic maps as an aid to locating likely nesting structures. There is no substitute for systematic visual inspection, and the falconer should examine all prospective formations until finding the one the falcons have selected. Many cliffs have a "magnetic" property that attracts falcons to nest there each year, although the chosen nest ledge or specific nest site may differ from one year to the next. High vertical faces and deep fissures offer the greatest protection from mammalian predators. While some eyries hang conspicuously from the cliff face like a painting, many more are tucked away into some secret crevice, chimney, or hole. In any particular year, the falconer may be required to spend considerable time watching the falcons' activities on the cliffs to determine the actual location of the eyrie. It is equally important to examine carefully all stick nests located on a cliff. Hawks, eagles, ravens, and owls often share or alternate occupancy on lines of cliffs with prairie falcons. While prairie falcons are not known to engage actively in nest building, they often take over abandoned stick nests for their own.

The best way to discover an eyrie is to find a comfortable spot with a good view of the cliff and to sit quietly. One must be far enough from the cliff so as not to upset the adults, but close enough to pinpoint the eyrie location with binoculars or a spotting scope. The observer may expect to witness some dramatic sights while trying to locate a nesting site. Wild falcons racing along the face of a cliff can be spectacular. The courting displays of the haggard tiercel wooing his mate qualify as aerobatic exhibitions of the finest order, and the fierce battles between resident falcons and intruders are equally impressive. These pleasant interludes are all-too-short breaks in what may otherwise be long hours of tedious searching. Incidentally, spells of inactivity often precede the visit of an adult bird to the nest ledge. In addition to incubating eggs, brooding, and feeding young, haggard falcons may be seen inspecting their eyries from time to time. These visits sometimes provide the only clues to an obscure eyrie location.

Early in the breeding season, adult falcons tend to sit tightly when incubating eggs or brooding young until annoyed or frightened off the nest ledge by noise. Thus, it is sometimes possible to mark eyrie locations by clapping your hands or shouting at the cliff and noting the point at which the adult leaves or returns to the cliff. For extremely tall cliffs or those far from the road or trail, one may resort to discharging a gun in the direction of the cliff. However, I prefer to use the least obtrusive means to relay my presence to the nesting falcons. Gunshots may also attract unwanted attention to your presence at an eyrie.

Remember, a falcon that is suddenly frightened from a nest at close range may break eggs or accidentally kick eggs or young off the nest ledge. Rather than panic the nesting falcon into flight, I think it wiser to move into a good position to observe the cliff, then begin to talk and shout, attempting to bring the falcon off the cliff with a minimum of disturbance. Particularly when it's early in the season, one should limit the amount of time that the adults are kept off the nest in order to prevent chilling of eggs and young.

A curious phenomenon is that falconers from some urban areas traditionally take birds from one or two well-known eyries. Repeated disturbance of the falcons' breeding efforts can lead to nest abandonment. There are enough cases of persistent birdwatchers and photographers causing nest failure among raptors to warrant concern. Expend the effort to find new eyries in out-of-the-way places. This is a satisfying accomplishment and one that helps guarantee that there will be an eyas in the eyrie when you are ready to collect it.

Later in the season, it may also be possible to find an eyrie by walking along the base of the cliff. Mutes are often present below the eyrie and swarms of flies are sometimes attracted to the food debris on the nest ledge. One should also listen for sounds from the young. Eyasses call out as the adults fly by the cliff and occasionally scold ravens, hawks, eagles, or vultures that wander by the eyrie.

Obviously, it will be much easier to find the eyrie and take an eyas if the falconer has at least one other person to act as an assistant. It is also much safer! Although the falconer may be able to accomplish the initial tasks of the search alone, one should never attempt to do any climbing when unassisted. It is particularly helpful to have observers located both above and below the nest ledge. Persons walking along the top of the cliff may be in an ideal position to spot a falcon leaving the eyrie or to prod an adult bird into flight. They may also be able to identify the best point on the cliff for rappelling to the nest ledge. It is often impossible to see the eyrie from above, however, and it is occasionally difficult to locate the exact position above the eyrie where the rope should be placed. Two-way radios will aid in this process, and are strongly recommended. The people above and below the cliff should expect to have communication problems under the best conditions, and a windy day will only make things worse. Referees' whistles used with prearranged coded signals provide a helpful backup method for exchanging messages.

After finding the prairie falcon eyrie, the falconer normally collects an eyas by rappelling to the nest ledge. Among seasoned rock climbers, rappelling is regarded as one of the most dangerous maneuvers. Rappelling is fun and deceptively simple, which may put the climber off guard. Despite continuing innovations in the design of their equipment, a number of climbers are injured or killed every year as a result of their own miscalculations. Falconers who value their longevity will want to make every effort to learn about rock climbing techniques and equipment. These lessons should be completed ahead of the eyas-taking season. Before flinging oneself over a cliff to

Acquiring a Falcon

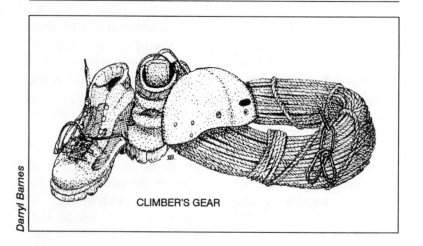
CLIMBER'S GEAR
Darryl Barnes

take a young bird from its nest, the falconer must know how to use the equipment and have practical experience on ropes. No amount of enthusiasm will make up for a lack of good judgment and climbing experience; dangling on a rope hundreds of feet above the ground is no place to discover that rappelling is not really one's cup of tea! If the falconer is acrophobic or unable to prepare in time, he or she should engage the assistance of a skilled climber.

I strongly suggest the systematic use of an equipment checklist in preparing for rock climbing tasks. My recommended list of essential items is as follows:

Climbers Checklist

1. Two approved climbing ropes of 1/2-inch or 11-millimeter diameter, one for rappelling and one for belaying (safety line). Lengths of 150 feet are adequate for most cliffs.
2. Protective climbing helmet and leather gloves.
3. Six each—standard and locking carabineers.
4. Figure "8" ring—friction descending device.
5. Two or more 20-foot sections of 1-inch tubular nylon webbing for fashioning rappelling seat harness. Com-

mercially made harnesses are available and diaper slings may also be used.
6. Several slings made of 1-inch tubular nylon webbing. Circles of the webbing are made in different diameters for use in setting protection.

Optional devices include: referee's whistles, chest harness, ascending devices such as "Jumars," and two-way radios.

When rigging for the descent to the nest ledge, it is always reassuring to know that the rope is firmly and securely attached to some immovable object such as a tree or boulder. A bowline knot should be used to tie off at the top of the cliff. If there is no large, heavy object readily available close to the edge of the cliff, it will be necessary to improvise. On such occasions, my friends and I have tied off to truck axles, metal bars driven into the ground, pitons, slings, chocks, sagebrush, or a combination of similar objects, for lack of something better. Once the rope is secure at the top, the harnesses and equipment can be attached. After all items are thoroughly checked and double checked, the climber can cautiously begin rappelling down to the eyrie, assisted by the person tending the belaying line. Throughout the descent, the climber must be alert for any hazards. Falling rocks jarred loose by the climber or by the rope slapping against the scree on the cliff surface can be especially dangerous, as well as sharp edges that can cut the ropes. In situations where falling rocks could endanger the eggs or young in an exposed eyrie, the climber should plan to rappel parallel to the eyrie and swing onto the nest ledge. Again, a word of caution: Never climb alone!

Eyasses can be transported to the ground by means of a small backpack; a wicker basket insert will provide added safety for the eyas. In situations where it is easier to ascend the cliff from the eyrie than to rappel to the bottom, one may thus have both hands unfettered. Should the climber slip, there is less chance of squashing the eyas between one's body and the cliff when transporting it on one's back. For the trip home, a cardboard box with wall-to-wall carpet serves well. This gives the unsteady eyas something to grip when being moved and helps prevent splaying of the legs. Leg splaying, caused when the eyas is left on a flat, smooth surface, will permanently injure or ruin an eyas if left uncorrected.

5 Preflight for Falconers

> Constant and total vigilance is the price of keeping a hawk right.
> —*Alva G. Nye, Jr.*

The task of taming and training a game hawk commences as soon as the falconer acquires a falcon. The falconer and the newly acquired raptor must start to develop an amicable relationship and dissolve any distrust between them. This is where the fun begins!

Ground school and flying lessons are essential steps in the training of a game hawk, but these lessons can't begin until the raptor learns to respond to the falconer. If one is to succeed in getting the falcon's undivided attention, one must first provide for its health and well-being, calm its fears, and persuade it to accept the falconer as a partner. Whether eyas or passager, the falconer must begin immediately to build a bond of special trust and confidence with the falcon. Proper food, shelter, and tender, loving care are primary considerations in this initial stage, but there are a number of essential supporting actions that contribute directly to a healthy and constructive relationship between the falconer and new game hawk.

There is a profound bit of aviation wisdom that says: "Flying in itself is not inherently dangerous, but it is mercilessly unforgiving of human error." The same advice applies to falconry.

HAWK FOOD

When I was getting started as a falconer in the early 1960s, the standard diet for trained raptors consisted of beef heart, stew beef, and horse meat. It is no wonder that so many hawks and falcons of that era were malnourished. Foot problems were common, and the absence of bones in the diet meant that beaks needed continual coping. Day-old cockerels became the next hawk food fad, but alone they also lacked the proper components of a balanced diet. Pigeons have long been considered a good diet for most hawks, and some falconers still raise, buy, or trap them as food for their birds. Unfortunately, pigeons carry diseases that can prove fatal to birds of prey. Today, we know that a clean, whole-bird diet is essential for maintaining captive falcons in top condition.

The two best sources of maintenance food for trained raptors are chickens and quail. Day-old cockerels of the laying breeds may be acquired for little or nothing from hatcheries. These can be raised easily in a simple poultry brooder for six weeks before being killed and frozen. While raising cockerels is inexpensive, they tend to be messy and there is some waste to the carcass.

Currently, the general falconry community is beginning to understand what a few individual falconers and raptor breeders discovered some time ago; Coturnix quail are an ideal food for captive birds of prey of all sizes. These quail possess a light but palatable flesh, and they are as clean a food source as may be found. Coturnix quail, otherwise known as Pharaoh or Japanese quail, are produced in huge numbers annually for food and research purposes, and they are easy to raise. The prolific hens lay more eggs in a year than a chicken, and the quail reach full size and sexual maturity in eight weeks. Aside from their food value, one of the greatest advantages for falconry is that hundreds of these birds can be raised in a small area with minimum effort.

A single Coturnix quail is the perfect-sized food package for falconry. One quail provides an adequate meal for a prairie falcon with very little excess. This is ideal because leftover food kept in a refrigerator for several days can cause the malady known as "sour crop," even without the slightest suggestion of spoilage. The problem of sour crop need never arise if the falcon is fed only fresh or freshly thawed food. I've also discovered that it is seldom necessary to cope a falcon that feeds on small, whole birds each day. A natural diet hones the beak.

Quail reach the optimum size for hawk food at forty-five days of age. Blood lines of quail reflect an assortment of sizes and colors, so one will have to choose the quail best suited for one's needs.

By raising one's own hawk food, the falconer is able to vary the nutritional content of the falcon's diet according to the falcon's needs. For instance, a 4- to 5-week-old quail is not mature, and its flesh is quite lean. Because it has not accumulated body fat, it is quickly passed through the falcon after being consumed. Such food is fully nutritious but is akin to a high quality washed meat that may be used to fill up a game hawk without filling it out. On the other hand, a falcon will gain weight on a diet of quail older than eight weeks because the quail are larger and fatter. The older quail are fine feed for flying hawks in cold weather or for molting birds, but they should not be used when the falconer wants to get the hawk's attention. Such subtleties often come into play, particularly when one is training imprints. Imprinted falcons need to feel full after every meal, but they should not necessarily be fed a rich diet that would render them totally unresponsive in warm weather.

A variety of food is important for providing captive raptors with a balanced diet. There is however, justifiable concern that many wild sources of hawk food available today may be contaminated by pollutants of various types. In my opinion, it is prudent to rely on the safest food sources available. In any case, game hawks will probably have ample opportunity to kill and consume several different species of prey over the course of the hunting season, and their success in the field will contribute to the variety of their food intake. To ensure that raptors are receiving proper and complete nutrition, vitamin supplements may be added occasionally to the quail carcass prior to feeding.

MEWS, PERCHES, AND JESSES

Most readers of this book are probably familiar with Murphy's Laws. His famous first law is simple, straightforward, and universal: If anything can go wrong, it will. Our noble sport has not been exempted from his edicts. I know for a fact that Mr. Murphy is alive, well, and still active somewhere within the North American falconry community. When it comes to finding examples of Murphy's Laws in falconry, there is simply no place like home!

All captive falcons will spend a great deal of time on a perch or block. Unfortunately, falcons will eventually become tangled when tied to any type of perch. To my knowledge, more birds of prey have died by accident on screen perches than on any other design. For this reason, I never use them. For use indoors, either the shelf perch or a round perch is preferred. I strongly favor leaving a falcon loose in a chamber when the falconer cannot be on hand to watch the bird.

For one falcon of any size, a chamber measuring 10-feet long, 8-feet wide, and 7-feet high is adequate and serviceable. I prefer to have a large window facing east to catch the morning sun; a large window also promotes good air circulation. A double door safety entrance is essential, and either screened louvers or a side window will be needed for ventilation in the summer. I install vertical bars on the windows that are spaced every inch and a half; this is adequate for restraining tiercel peregrines or prairie falcons but smaller raptors need bars spaced no wider than 1 1/4 inch. Padded shelf perches are needed near the windows (slanted cocomat perches work well) and I also build a perch or ledge higher up on the rear wall. Both perches and ledges should allow the falcon a cushioned landing surface of adequate size and should present no obstacle to a bird in flight. All studs must be covered and there should be nothing for the falcon to hit or snag while flying around inside

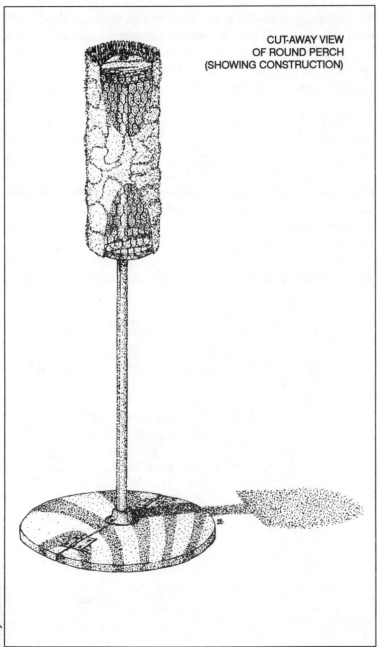

CUT-AWAY VIEW
OF ROUND PERCH
(SHOWING CONSTRUCTION)

the enclosure. Obviously, the floor of the chamber must allow for a soft landing. I have used sand, pea gravel, and wood chips but prefer pea gravel. If a chamber is built on the ground, 1/4-inch pea gravel is best for drainage. Any floor material will require regular cleaning to prevent a buildup of potentially dangerous bacteria.

A chamber of this size provides enough space for a gyrfalcon to move around, but it is not so long that a falcon can build up any real speed within its confines.

Thus, the falcon is not likely to be injured by flying into a wall or onto a perch. The same chamber can serve as a free loft during the molt or as a safe nursery for an eyas. It is also small enough that a reluctant imprint in a playful mood may not long escape its place on the fist.

Block size and jess length are also important factors affecting the safety of captive raptors. A good rule of thumb for block

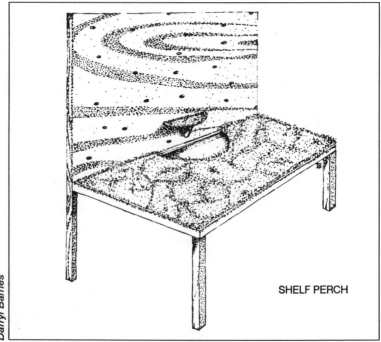

SHELF PERCH

safety is that the width of the block top should exceed the length of the jess. For female prairie falcons and peregrines, a block diameter of seven inches is sufficient. Gyrfalcons, sakers, and large hybrids will require a block with an 8-inch top. For all large falcons, I suggest a jess length of six inches. Tiercel prairies and peregrines are better accommodated on a 6-inch block with jesses of 5 1/2 inches in length. These dimensions are conservative and should prevent the falcon from straddling the block. Block straddling occurs when the jesses slip down opposite sides of the block and snub the falcon to the post, a situation that results in disaster.

For birds that are blocked out all day, particularly during the molt, stiff leashes and jess extenders are a good precaution.

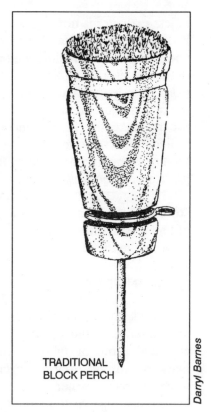
TRADITIONAL BLOCK PERCH

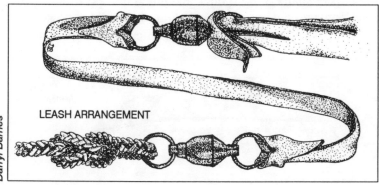
LEASH ARRANGEMENT

82 Preflight for Falconers

A jess extender is nothing more than a 6-inch strip of leather with a slit cut in each end. The jesses are threaded through one end of the extender while the other end is attached to the ring of the swivel. The object is to keep the button on the end of the leash from getting caught between the jesses and tangling up the falcon; the extender also permits the use of shorter jesses. I use the extender in conjunction with a nylon leash that is braided onto the opposing ring of the swivel. While this leash has no button to contend with, the extender aids in keeping the jesses free of both swivel and leash.

In many respects, the extender functions like an Arabic "tubloca," a leash and jess arrangement, with the double action of the jesses rotating within the Aylmeri grommets and the swivel set in the leash.

BROKEN FEATHERS

Accidental damage to a falcon's feathers is an infrequent consequence of the falconry regime. This could probably be classified as one of the occupational hazards to which a game hawk is exposed. Any damaged feather warrants immediate attention; each feather is supported by its neighbor so that gaps leave them unprotected. Bent feathers may be restored quickly to full use by applying warm water through dipping or spraying.

Broken feathers must be imped. Traditionally, the feather is cut at the break and metal or wooden pins are inserted into the hollow shafts of both ends and glued into position. Epoxy glue, contact cement, and Super Glue have all been used for this purpose. Another technique is to cut the feather at the

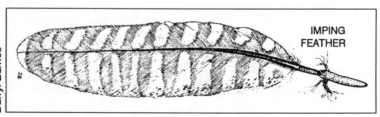
IMPING FEATHER
Darryl Barnes

break and fashion a replacement feather so that it slides into the hole in the shaft. The overlapping junction of the feathers is then sewn and glued into place. Because the broken end of the feather cannot always be reused, many falconers maintain a store of molted feathers for use in emergencies.

The best method I've used for repairing broken feathers involves the use of a cyanoacrylate adhesive (trade name ZAP/-CA) and pins made of bamboo. Although midfeather breaks can be repaired, I prefer to imp the feather near the base of the shaft using an intact feather of matching size and shape. In my experience, this method is more effective than splicing the broken feather in stress areas where it is likely to break again. The broken quill is cut off approximately 1 1/2 inches from the base and matched with the replacement feather. Next, a bamboo pin about one inch in length is shaved so that it will fit inside the quill without splitting the shaft. Then, with the glue applied, the pin is inserted into the end of the replacement feather. The application of a spray (trade name ZAP KICKER) hardens the liquid glue instantly and eliminates the mess and sticky feathers associated with imping. With the first bond secure, more glue is applied to the exposed end of the pin. This, in turn, is inserted into the remnant end of the broken feather and held in place until hardened by the spray. By imping a whole feather this way, it is possible to provide a replacement feather, in some cases stronger than the original, which will hold until the molt.

These new chemicals make it possible to put down layers of glue at imping joints for extra strength and to form strong bonds on badly split shafts. One may even prevent imping in the first place by strengthening bent feathers with a layer or two of glue before more serious damage occurs.

Care must be taken when restraining raptors for imping as they become stressed and overheated during this kind of handling. In multiple feather repairs or with a particularly high-strung bird, it may be safer to have a competent veterinarian anesthetize the bird to facilitate the imping process.

Under no circumstances should a broken feather be pulled out of a falcon. There is an extremely high risk of permanent damage to the feather follicle with such abuse. A damaged follicle may never again regenerate a normal feather.

THE LURE

The lure is an essential tool of the falconer and serves as the vital communication link with the game hawk. Used throughout the training and hunting phases of falconry, the lure is both an instrument of persuasion and a safety device. One of its most important applications is to enable the falconer to recall the bird promptly from a threatening or dangerous situation. Accordingly, the bird must be conditioned from the outset to associate the lure with something positive and fascinating. The concept of lure-training falcons was discussed in J. G. Mavrogordato's work, *A Falcon In The Field*. In it, he stated, "each action must have one, and only one, significance." This is a key concept to bear in mind. The lure should signify only one thing to a falcon; the end of the flight.

Whether the falcon is raised with the lure or introduced to it later in life, the lure should represent all that is good. A falcon may be taught to respond to any distinctive object—even an old shoe—so long as the bird learns to recognize the object as a source of food. Some of the strange and weird contraptions that falconers have dreamed up to train hawks will prove my point. For example, most nineteenth century falconry literature recommended the use of a padded horse shoe for a lure. I never did try it, and I can't imagine anyone swinging such a potentially dangerous object in front of a hardhitting falcon!

A serviceable lure can be made by sewing two pieces of leather together with foam rubber padding in between. I make lures approximately 10-inches long and 4-inches wide so that they fit easily into my hawking bag. Attached to the top of the lure are strings for securing food, a swivel for rotation, and a line and drag weight of approximately eight ounces. Shapes vary and I have seen lure designs in ovals, hearts, horseshoes, and even artificial ducks. While lures are easy to make, there is one over-the-counter product that serves quite well. It is the retrieving dummy used for training puppies. This inexpensive item is made of washable canvas, is light in weight, and floats. The dummy can easily be fitted with a line and weight and fashioned into an extremely durable lure. Bird wings or leather flaps may be attached if desired, but such features are of little value for an eyas.

I am inclined to question the worth of sophisticated lure designs, chiefly because I do not stoop falcons to the lure. Consequently, there is no need for any internal moving parts in my lures or for special precautions to prevent the falcon from accidental injury while hitting the lure. Sophisticated designs may have merit, but I find them of little use in game hawking.

Some falconers prefer to use "dead lures" consisting of intact bird bodies. A falcon responds well to these natural lures, although it may be inclined to ignore other types of lures after being spoiled on dead lures. I find it more convenient to feed fresh parts of birds to the falcon off the lure rather than using large carcasses as lures on a daily basis. Currently, I use a dead quail affixed to my lure. Quail make a handy-sized food package, and the falcon can be fed a complete meal off the lure and yet learns to come to the lure rather than just to the carcass. Likewise, a falcon will return to an ungarnished lure once the association is made between coming to the lure and being fed promptly from the fist.

BAGGED GAME

Bagged game, generally acquired from a game farm, is used to introduce the falcon to unfamiliar quarry. Technically, bagged game includes any bird that is artificially served for the falcon to catch. Whether it is served from a catapult, by hand, or planted before a flight, the bagged bird seldom has the appearance or flight style of a wild bird; usually these birds fly poorly and are easily captured. (The exceptions would be freshly trapped birds such as starlings.) Nevertheless, the use of bagged game is an especially effective technique for giving an eyas a good impression about some particular bird. When convinced that the new quarry can be killed and that it tastes good, the falcon will become interested in chasing it.

As a wild raptor, an eyas falcon learns to hunt young birds during the late summer. Obviously, that would be the ideal time to start presenting a captive eyas with hunting opportunities. It is noteworthy that the traditional opening of the red grouse season in Great Britain occurs on August 12th. Formerly, falconry seasons began much later in most parts of the United States and hunting regulations precluded early training of eyasses on wild game birds. Extended seasons now allow hawks and falcons to be trained on young game before the start of the shooting season and reduce the chances that a wayward eyas will be shot by some overzealous gunner.

In order to compensate for the starting dates of hunting seasons and late migrations of waterfowl, some North American falconers augment the training of their birds by using bagged game. The early season is a formative period for any eyas, and a falcon's career can be made or marred within its first two months of hunting. Ducks sometimes present a trying situation, as some falcons show no initial interest in them. A few bad experiences at this point may discourage the falcon from pursuing ducks or any other game. With proper presentation of bagged quarry, the falcon's reaction to an unfamiliar game bird can be positively influenced.

To be of value for entering purposes, upland game birds should be raised in large flight pens where they can fly. Similarly, ducks should be hacked to ensure that they will actually fly when released. Most commercially raised game birds simply have no muscle tone. They can be used to reward the falcon for good behavior, but can be counted on to fly only a minimal distance. In any event, the use of bagged game is typically restricted to the early part of the season.

The drawback to using bagged game is that the falcon learns that relentless pursuit pays off. Not only does this cause the falcon to abandon waiting-on, but long flights away from the falconer may mean the loss of the game hawk. Neither are to be encouraged. Flights at game and the use of highly trained homing pigeons will prevent or cure these faults over time.

Keeping in mind that a game hawk should be trained and made to wild quarry in a timely fashion, bagged game should be viewed as a brief interlude in this process. Consider the need for such birds carefully and use the minimum number (less than six) for entering purposes.

PIGEONS

I believe that a flock of homing pigeons is a great advantage for anyone training a falcon. Pigeons are a substitute for game birds and can be used to provide the falcon with flights throughout the year. Homing pigeons quickly learn the most effective actions for evading the falcon, and they return to the loft to be used again. This eliminates the drudgery of trapping feral pigeons that may expose the falcon and falconer to various diseases.

A good flock of racing pigeons is easy to establish. Young pigeons should be acquired about six months prior to obtaining the falcon, thus providing ample time to train the pigeons slowly and to allow them to mature before facing the falcon. During this period, it is advantageous for the pigeons to interact with wild raptors in order to gain a healthy respect for predators. The flock will require proper care to maintain their health and ensure their suitability as food for the falcon in case they are caught. For this reason, feral pigeons should never be allowed to mix with a groomed flock of racing pigeons.

I suggest buying inexpensive homing pigeons and training them methodically. A flock of thirty should be adequate. This number will allow for losses to natural mortality and attrition during the training flights, while still providing enough birds to last through the hawking season. At season's end, there should be enough remaining birds to repopulate the loft by the next fall.

Once the flock has been "settled" to the loft, the birds should be road-trained several times each week. For the month prior to using them in the falcon's training, the pigeons should be released fifty miles from home at least once a week. The objective is to have the birds at the peak of condition well before they see the falcon. When released for a prairie falcon, the pigeons should be served in open country; they should bypass cover when being pursued by the falcon. Untrained homers and barn pigeons often lack the strength or determination to outfly a falcon in the air, which is a major failing. While pigeons can shake off a peregrine by going to cover, a prairie falcon will kill them if they attempt to land. Therefore, it is critically important to use only the strongest pigeons as training aids in order to make the falcon work. A prairie falcon will quickly learn to press even top-quality homers to the limit.

Early in the season, any falcon may be expected to kill the few inexperienced pigeons that instinctively go for cover. But only those pigeons that go up, outfly the falcon, and leave the field climbing at top speed will survive the experience. These survivors will also make the best breeding stock in the coming spring. After killing a few weak pigeons, the falcon may begin to chase them out of sight; this can present a serious problem. I know of several instances in which prairie falcons have killed pigeons five miles from where the flight began. Not only did the pigeon fail to escape, but the falcon failed to learn that tail chasing is futile. The objective is to teach the falcon to fly properly, and it should never have the opportunity to catch a pigeon without striking it in the air first.

A cautionary note: strong pigeons and hard-flying falcons can make a dangerous combination, particularly in enclosed country. Even with radio transmitters, an errant falcon can become lost or killed when separated from the falconer for any length of time. Situations vary and each falconer must determine, perhaps through trial and error or controlled experiments, if this technique will truly benefit the falcon in question within the hawking space available. This is one of those crucial situations in which common sense must rule.

6 Training the Eyas

The falconer who acquires an eyas has every reason to anticipate a long and rewarding association with a dependable game hawk. In return for a reasonable investment in time and patience, one can expect the young eyas to learn the role of the reliable hunting falcon and to serve the falconer with loyal performance in the field. Two separate approaches are presented for dealing with imprinted and nonimprinted eyasses.

In training falcons, one applies the maximum amount of manipulation while minimizing the falcon's inhibitions. Most of what we know about training raptors is based on diet control, and many aspects of training may become the direct result of manipulation of food. For instance, eyasses will respond to the lure as a toy, irrespective of food. In addition, they can be taught to fly to the glove without food. By offering the glove to the eyas frequently as it sits on a low perch, it learns to respond—an extension of its innate desire to be at a higher level relative to its surroundings. More and more, falconers are learning to manipulate the natural propensities of falcons, eyas and passage, to falconry ends.

IMPRINTS

Most falcons are flying in less than seven weeks from the day they hatch. Because an eyas grows and changes rapidly, its training is a dynamic process. As the eyas passes through the stages of infancy, fledging, flying, and hunting, the falconer guides it, exerting influence at specific times. Each stage of development is a precursor to the next.

A falcon taken for training before it is three weeks of age is extremely fragile. These birds begin to thermoregulate or control their own body temperature when 10-days old, but require brooding before gaining their feathers. Young falcons from day-olds to large downies may be warmed with small still-air brooders, heat lamps, or with a temperature-controlled heating pad installed on the floor beneath a layer of towels or litter. It is essential that the falcon be kept out of drafts and that it be able to move close to a heat source when cold and away from heat when too hot. Constant observation is crucial. If taken at only a few days old, the falcon needs even closer attention to ensure that its legs do not become splayed. The tiny falcon must be kept on a firm but irregular surface to allow its feet to grip the floor area, thereby keeping its legs beneath its body. To keep the young bird on a smooth surface could result in malformed legs. One may use a layer of pea gravel one to two inches deep or a bed of corn cob litter on the floor of the brooder or box. Alternatively, a floor of rumpled-up cloths and towels makes an adequate substrate. However, the eyas should be neither too hot nor cold when so confined.

Feeding The Imprint

Falcons should be raised and maintained on a fresh whole-bird diet. Two-month-old Coturnix quail and five-week-old chickens (cockerels) make excellent hawk food and are easy to raise. Until eyasses are 2-weeks old, bird carcasses should be skinned, with the head, viscera, and scaly part of the legs and the feet removed, before the body is chopped with a meat cleaver or shears. Quartered parts of the body, minus the lower back and large ball joints, may then be run through a household meat grinder. Young falcons less than 10- to 12-days old require some help in eating and may be fed tiny pieces of meat from forceps or hemostats until they learn to reach for their meals. Downies will feed themselves from a shallow dish if food is left close by. Some people prefer to have eyasses feed themselves from a dish, while others like the hand-feeding method. It matters little which method is used as long as the falcon is fed all it cares to eat at a sitting. Food should be left for an eyas to eat between scheduled feedings. One advantage to feeding falcons from a dish is that they become accustomed to picking at their food, making an easy transition to feeding themselves from a carcass. It is also possible to begin feeding small downies ground meat from the lure so that they learn the correct association with it at a tender age.

The most important concept to remember with imprints is that food should always be available in *unlimited* quantity. The dish or lure should represent the "horn of plenty" to an eyas. As falcons develop, they will eat larger amounts of food at fewer meals. One must let the falcon's appetite and behavior dictate the quantity and frequency of feedings. When the falcon begins to approach a certain mealtime with indifference, or ignores it completely, the time is probably right to eliminate the meal gradually. Eyasses less than 2-weeks old eat about every three hours between 6:00 A.M. and 10:00 P.M. From ages two to four weeks, they eat between four and six meals in the same time period. Appetites of eyasses 4- to 6-weeks old wane to three large meals daily. Eyasses 6- to 10-weeks of age are conditioned to two meals daily, and for older eyasses a single meal will suffice.

Ideally, the eyas should discover food in a variety of places. Once the bird is mobile (4- to 5-weeks of age), jumping out of its box or bassinet and running around, food is placed wherever the eyas may be. At this stage, I offer quail carcasses in an attempt to wean the eyas off ground meat. Meals should be taken in the presence of people, dogs, and commotion. I find it easier to preplace food and bring the eyas to it, rather than make the food magically appear in front of the bird. This may also be accomplished by hooding the falcon, laying out the food, removing the hood and allowing the falcon to go to it and eat.

Before the falcon can fly, a table is a good place for feeding, as the bird is close to eye level with everyone. But as an eyas becomes mobile, it should be fed on the floor or ground. Once the eyas learns to look for the garnished lure or a carcass, the food may be placed in plain view for the falcon to find. Early on, I like to feed an eyas on the kitchen floor so that it becomes accustomed to people and dogs walking around while it eats.

If carefully fed and handled the young falcon will not be anxious about people approaching it in the field. Given the number of meals that the eyas will take off the floor or ground in this manner, the falconer should be able to assess its potential as a carrier: a falcon that flies away with its food. Barring poor handling or an unforeseen accident, the eyas should feel no need to carry. Because it will always be fed all it wants, it should neither mantle nor scream when with food. Ground food cannot be carried and solid food tied to a lure should be made too difficult for an eyas to pull or carry very far. Likewise, carcasses may be secured if there is some reason to believe the eyas will bolt with the food if given the opportunity. A certain amount of jumping around and mock attacks on food are to be expected from an eyas. Running about the floor with a lure or bird in its foot does not necessarily indicate that the falcon is carrying. If the falconer is concerned, the food may be attached to a board or weighted line, which will prevent the falcon from going far with the meal.

Any time that feeding takes place out-of-doors, the food item must be secured to a weight or drag. Indoors, the food does not necessarily need to be weighted. When feeding after hacking periods, the eyas should be well into the meal, perhaps having consumed half a crop of food, before the falconer reaches in to secure its jesses. Just as when it actually catches quarry, the falcon will be particularly anxious about being approached until it has "killed" and commenced to eat. If the jesses are secured slowly and deliberately, the falcon should ignore the action and continue eating. The end of the leash must be secured in a manner that will prevent the falcon from flying away once it has finished its meal. When the falcon is finished

EYAS PRAIRIE FALCON

Darryl Barnes

eating, it will step off the lure or carcass and begin feaking or cleaning its beak. This is when the falconer should offer the fist to the falcon and encourage it to step up on the glove. The leash is then removed from its drag, wound up, and the falcon permitted to finish feaking on the glove before being hooded.

There may be a long period after the falcon has begun to fly during which it will still require feeding more than once a day. At first, it should be fed a full crop of food during all meals. When it is finally cut down to two feedings a day, it should still be fed all it wants at the morning meal. Then, gradually and slowly, the amount of food offered in the morning is reduced and eventually eliminated. However, the falcon may want at least a snack in the morning for a month or two after its feathers have become hard-penned. The falcon's behavior is the best measuring tool that one has through this adjustment process. If the falcon begins to scream or mantle, the change in feeding is probably going too quickly and the falconer should restore generous food portions for awhile. After the falcon begins flying, I prefer to feed the morning meal on the floor of the falcon's chamber. Not only does this allow me to spend more time in watching the bird, but I may observe the degree of anxiety with which the falcon approaches its meal. This indicates how concerned the falcon may be with its food on any particular day. Because the eyas always receives all it wants at the evening meal, its behavior at the morning feeding can serve as a guide for judging the pace at which the falcon should be weaned from this meal.

The falconer should be present at every meal the eyas falcon takes until it is proven in the field, even if this means simply sitting in the chamber while the eyas takes its morning meal from the lure. Modern life places many demands on one's time, but sacrifices must be made if one wants a bird that won't even consider carrying a sparrow should it catch one. As western falconers should have learned from our counterparts in the Middle East, there is no substitute for time spent manning a falcon. Imprints are notorious for taking a long time to eat, especially when learning to kill. A meal may last more than an hour from start to finish because the youngster pauses to consider whether or not to break into the kill. The falconer should relax and not rush the falcon, no matter how long the meal takes. Yanking away quarry from a self-indulgent eyas will surely be met with hostility. This type of handling not only encourages carrying, but screaming and mantling as well. Easygoing falcons will allow the falconer to help them open the kill, but one must use caution and avoid offending the eyas by getting in its way if it wants to act alone. The safer course is to allow the eyas to proceed at its own pace. One method to reduce the time spent in feeding is to slide precut pieces of meat, placed atop the lure, over to the falcon as it is engaged in eating. To train an imprint properly, one must accept the fact that the process will be painfully slow. Once the falcon learns, it will spend little time in playing with a hard-earned meal.

Handling the Imprint

The imprint may be handled at any time *except* when it is eating. Eyasses resent anything separating them from their food. Hooding lessons should take place before each meal; there should be no need to draw the braces on the hood fully until the falcon becomes nearly hard-penned. Tidbitting the falcon, a useful technique with wild-caught hawks, is unnecessary with these birds. To attempt to make friends with an eyas in such a manner may send conflicting signals; the bird ultimately may become a screamer.

Downies may be carried easily but need to be well-supported, as they become insecure when being lifted and transported. Small downies may be carried in one's hand, but larger birds should be carried in a box or basket that provides them with adequate footing. This prevents a young falcon from panicking and falling to the floor because it fears being dropped. For eyasses 2- to 4-weeks old, this is a fearful stage and carrying should be avoided. Once feathered out, the eyas will grip the glove and ride comfortably. If the eyas is rambunctious, it should be hooded while being carried to prevent bating.

Socialization is a continuing, long-term process and should be maintained throughout the falcon's life. Just as the imprint needs food, it needs love and attention to remain well-adjusted. The key is to spend time with the bird and expose it to the hustle and bustle of life around it. This is sometimes an inconvenience for the household, as the falcon initially sheds a considerable amount of down and may deposit an occasional mute in unwanted places. But such inconvenience is a small price to pay for a bird that will be a prize when it finishes school.

Like most youngters, eyasses are stimulus addicts. Although they spend a considerable amount of time sleeping, they crave activity and need to act when the mood strikes them. This is one reason why the falconer must spend time with the eyas and must be involved with every aspect of its life. One should devote time to play periods and also provide toys for play while no one is around. Little rubber "squeaky" toys, lures, tennis balls, rolled-up newspapers, and the like are favorites with eyasses. They will pounce on and chew these toys in mock attacks that may keep them occupied for hours. One wants a falcon that is totally tame, yet responds positively to its surroundings before it grows up. The habits learned during these formative periods will last a lifetime.

I have found that a large cardboard box (2 feet x 3 feet) serves well as a crib for the young falcon. If the top half of the front piece is bent to make a moveable flap, the top corners can be taped or tied to create a window that folds down to allow easy access to the bird for feeding. Strings secure the flap in the "up" position. In addition, I cut slots in the folding piece, which give the moveable portion a barred appearance. This allows the falconer to see in and the falcon to see out during times when it should remain inside the box. Bedding, in the form of old towels or sheets, should be removed every other day and washed. Of course, this period in its life is short; the eyas will be popping up to the edge of the box and fluttering out in a matter of weeks. One can prolong the use of the box by folding up the lid or placing a light towel over the top during periods when the bird should remain inside.

A plexiglass box, or half a large sky kennel equipped with a 1/8-inch clear plastic or lexan sheet to block the opening, has added advantages. It allows the eyas visual access to its surroundings and, in turn, allows its activities to be monitored. In addition, these items are durable and easily cleaned. Regular cleaning improves hygiene and reduces indoor odor. This is particularly important for falconers (and breeders) who raise numerous eyasses.

After the eyas has passed the box stage, it will spend its time either loose in its chamber or tied to a block in the weathering yard. At night, I prefer to keep eyasses inside. One eyas even slept regularly on top of the dresser in my bedroom. An indoor block, round perch, or shelf perch is more convenient, however. Watching an eyas go through all of its morning rituals can be entertaining. After feeding it indoors or in the chamber, I like to loose the eyas in the chamber so that it may pump its wings, run around, and work off its youthful energy. Then, after this bit of "free time," I put it out on a block to weather.

All birds of prey feel most comfortable on the highest perch available. An eyas that is left to its own devices indoors will inevitably find its way to the top of a bookshelf or similar lookout. A tame eyas is a pleasant sight late in the evening, preening and stretching, without a care in the world. One may relax and enjoy its company, provided that the drapes are drawn, the doors remain closed, and newspapers are judiciously applied. And, like "child proofing" a house, there is a need to secure fragile moveable items. While some falcons rest comfortably on such roosts, others are too active to be trusted to sit quietly when untethered. The time will come when the eyas must be confined to a perch that will permit it to be around civilized company without endangering itself by its desire to fly.

By the time an eyas is feathered and running about, it should be trained to the block. By starting with a small car tire, laid flat so that the tire is only six to eight inches off the ground, the falconer may encourage the eyas to jump up and perch. The leash is passed through the center of the tire and secured with a falconer's knot, or a hole may be cut in the sidewall of the tire to accommodate it. The first restraints of the leash are an unpleasant affair and the sooner the eyas accepts the tether, the better. By five or six weeks of age, the falcon should be well-accustomed to sitting on the block. The falcon will be unable to bate hard enough to hurt itself and will throw less of a tantrum if it is block trained early in life. I know of falconers who did not introduce their eyasses to a block until after the birds were tame hacked. The scenes that the falcons caused when first tied down were disquieting, to say the least.

Screaming

All falcons vocalize in social situations and screaming in imprints is often linked to recognition of the falconer and not necessarily related to food. With constant companionship and social interaction, the noise factor will be greatly reduced. Screaming from hunger is the direct result of poor management. In another category, some eyasses become conditioned screamers. This develops from boredom, lack of attention, poor handling technique, or a combination of social and hunger screaming.

The well-adjusted imprint does not know fear, insecurity, or loneliness because it grows up in a continual association with people. This includes the physical contact of being held in arms and laps when it is young. By design, imprints are denied a physical and mental relationship with siblings. Therefore, the falconer and other people must assume this role to instill a sound mental outlook in the youngster.

Lure Conditioning and Bird Training

Because the lure is the best communication link between the falconer and the bird, the falcon should learn to love it. Downies may be conditioned to know the lure from an early age, but knowledge of the lure is just as important for older eyasses. Fresh meat, preferably carcasses, should be attached to the lure. Falcons learn quickly that the lure represents food, yet some birds appear to pay little attention to the lure. For that reason, the falconer should give the eyas a subconscious reminder that the lure is, in fact, fascinating. This may be accomplished by attaching live quail to the lure and allowing the falcon to kill and eat the birds. If repeated several times, the falcon more likely will be fond of the lure than if the lure represents only cold meat after a flight.

In the same vein, a plump eyas may show little interest in catching or killing birds. One way to prime the falcon is to release half-grown quail in its chamber and allow the eyas to kill and eat what it wants. Even the fattest baby falcon cannot long resist the chance to pursue a young bird. Having once been primed, the eyas will pursue its prey readily, even though it may consume only a portion of the body at that time. In so doing, the instinct to hunt is aroused at an early age. If it is to be interested in pursuing prey, the eyas should feel the passions of a hunter.

Tame Hacking

Before an eyas can fly, the falconer may allow it to run around in a backyard or similarly enclosed area, with careful supervision. If the eyas is lure trained at this point, the lure may be presented for the eyas to find, play with, or feed from while romping in the grass. One may prefer to hold play periods in the field where the eyas will be hacked.

Once the eyas recognizes and comes to the lure or a carcass as a source of food, it is safe to begin the tame-hacking procedure. The objective is to allow the young falcon to learn to fly at its own pace and to develop its flying skills, after which it is enticed to return to the lure. Weight control has little to do with this activity. Flying becomes the activity that precedes the normal schedule of meals and the eyas returns to the lure more out of habit than hunger. The corpulent youngster may thus pursue its flying lessons about the center of activity that the falconer creates, while developing some degree of the homing instinct that returns it to that same place when physically spent.

The tame-hacking procedure is an integral part of the imprinted falcon's development, and teaches the bird to behave in a natural way. Imprints become accustomed to being around people and possess none of the innate suspicions of their wild counterparts. For this reason, the falconer is obliged to keep close watch over the imprint.

I prefer to raise and hack one falcon at a time. In my opinion, a falconer can produce a more secure bird with better manners when all of one's attention is focused on a single pupil. However, other falconers claim that their gang-hacking methods work well and that eyasses gain much stimulation from interacting at hack with other falcons. Nevertheless, such methods always pose the risk of encouraging defensive behavior in eyasses being fed in groups. Great care should be taken to separate the hack birds at feeding time. When four or five falconers are involved, each can be responsible for feeding his or her own bird. On the other hand, if one person is attempting to tame-hack two or more falcons, it is also advisable that the birds be visually separated while they eat.

In my experience, at least one eyas in a group inevitably is noisy. Even in the weathering yard, screaming may become contagious if an otherwise quiet falcon is subjected to such behavior for long. While I've been told that screaming birds generally stop after a year, I remain unconvinced. The potential bad habits learned through a group hack would seem to outweigh any merits of the technique. One may fly a falcon into condition, but screaming is a difficult, if not impossible, vice to correct.

Hacking periods should coincide with the time of day that the falconer expects to be hawking, so that the bird learns to anticipate flying at that particular time. While some falconers choose to fly their birds in the morning, this time tends to be more dangerous than afternoon or evening periods. Evening flights limit the amount of time and distance that a falcon may put between itself and the falconer, if the bird decides to stray. The warm thermals of late summer and early fall produce less seductive influences on the falcon if it is flown in the evening. In addition, the setting sun helps to focus the attention of the falcon, even if fat, on the notion of eating before dark. The urge to disperse from natal areas is particularly strong in young falcons during late August. The falconer must remain ever vigilant for signs of wanderlust.

The exuberant eyas is sure to make its own fun. Its activities may involve bedeviling some other bird into becoming a sparring partner for an evening's entertainment. Nearly anything may become "prey" for an eyas at hack. This willingness to chase anything for fun puts the falcon in good shape and helps the falconer prepare the bird for training. Since it is not hungry, the falcon is not actually hunting at this point. However, the falcon is interested in the birds it chases and feels the drive to hunt whether hungry or not. The stronger the falcon becomes, the more likely it will become a successful game hawk.

During these forays after "dickey" birds, the rudiments of falconry are laid. A falcon that is chasing birds for fun may return overhead at a modest pitch. A pigeon that is then served under the falcon is almost certain to be stooped, and the initial pursuit will spark the falcon to try again. It may return above the falconer several times in anticipation of being served a pigeon, before tiring and taking a perch. While the falcon may not be capable of catching pigeons at this stage, it is usually willing to chase them. Before long, the falcon will return from its jaunts to wait-on above the falconer, expecting that delectable but elusive pigeon to reappear. Because the hack should continue for four to five weeks, it is not necessary that the falcon be killing pigeons from the outset. Occasionally, one may serve an easy pigeon to encourage the falcon. A falcon at hack, like a wild eyas, is driven by instinct to pursue birds even though a small percentage of these sorties are successful. The falcon's weight contributes to its continuing, playful attitude toward life. At this stage, the falcon will be quite content to return to the lure for a relaxed meal after flying.

Falcons are known to develop a homing attraction for certain locations or structures on the hacking grounds. Some eyasses even "home" to their falconer's vehicle. One can envision that in the future, falconers will gain more understanding of this behavior and culture this instinct to a greater degree.

During the hacking period, several events transpire to affect the falcon's behavior. First, the falcon matures and gains confidence in the air. This confidence gradually translates into hunting aggression as the eyas encounters progressively more challenging prey. While this process is taking place, the falconer slowly reduces the falcon's food intake at the morning meal. As a result of these reductions, the bird's first pangs of hunger are likely to be felt at evening time, and its hunting attitude will be directly affected. This latter development is crucial. As the falcon gains strength and confidence, the falconer begins to exert control over the bird's wanderings. The falconer molds the falcon's behavior at this point by attempting to confine its flying activities to the airspace overhead and by rewarding its desire to wait-on. The falconer also influences the falcon's choice of prey by presenting the desired game for the falcon to hunt. These events should occur on a schedule that closely parallels the progress of a young wild falcon. As a rule, the imprint will be flying at tame-hack and learning to hunt at about the same stage of development as its wild counterpart.

Time Line For Development and Training of Imprinted Falcons		
Age (Weeks)	Category	Stage of Development and Training
0-2	Small Downy	Develops bonding, socialization, trust, etc., sits upright, eats ground food from dish.
3-4	Large Downy	Learns hood, feeds from lure, introduced to dog, car, and being approached.
5-6	Prefledging	Looks for lure, feeds from carcass, interacts with toys and people, attach jesses and dummy transmitter, block trained.
7-9	Fledging	Meals are scheduled and fed from lure, short flights, blocked during day.
10-12	Hack	Sustained flight, orients to falconer and location/structures, chases birds.
12	Enter	Begins to take pitch and wait-on, entered to pigeons and game, gains condition and stamina.

NONIMPRINTED EYASSES

Compared to imprints, older eyasses progress slowly through the various phases of training. The falconer must take extra time to tame these birds and overcome their fears. Consequently, such birds are in the field at a later date. They require longer periods to build condition, and typically learn to kill later than the imprint.

Falcons taken when they are more than 2-weeks old may show a greater fear of hands and handling than do younger birds. As a consequence, the falconer's initial efforts must be toward socialization. In order to ease it through its anxieties, the falcon should be handled often and be well-socialized.

The key to continued socialization is to keep the falcon in the mainstream of household activities. Repeated stroking, hooding, and carrying will alleviate the falcon's fear of hands. Like imprints, some older eyasses may seek companionship, whether perched nearby or in one's lap. However, a late-taken eyas is apt to foot and bite the falconer's hands when stroked. By using a rolled-up towel as a glove, the falconer can elevate and stroke the eyas. The bird will then be more concerned with holding onto its perch than with biting the falconer, and its fear of falling will prevent it from lashing out with its feet.

By keeping the falcon on an indoor perch in the evening and by weathering the bird during the day where it can watch the world go by, the falconer ensures that the falcon stays "involved." A falconer who is away from home during the day might consider making arrangements to leave the eyas at a kindergarten, though I've never heard of anyone doing so! Some falconers simply leave a T.V. set on to keep their eyasses company. However, this is no substitute for interactions with people. One falconer I know believes that an eyas should be constantly within sight of people and dogs until it is hard-penned. This individual goes so far as to hire a baby-sitter to be with his eyasses while he is at work. His eyasses do display excellent manners. By taking the falcon along on car trips, holding it bareheaded in the evening while relaxing, and including it in family activities, the falconer can produce the desired result. Few scenes are as gratifying as a beautifully mannered falcon sitting nonchalantly on a block while children and dogs romp on the floor nearby. Unfortunately, it is culturally unacceptable in this country to take trained falcons into public places. Both the falcons and the public would benefit from the exposure.

Fledged eyasses trapped two to three weeks off the nest (cliffers), traditionally hacked falcons, and captive-bred falcons reared in chambers until hard-penned, may be handled in essentially the same manner. By necessity, these birds must be manned like passage falcons. They should neither scream nor mantle. Of course, they will not have the worldly education of the late-taken passager. However, not all that a wild falcon learns is desirable for falconry. The fledged eyas gives the falconer an independent bird with good manners and few bad habits. These birds are available in early summer when days are long and the weather proves best for training. This is also the season when most falconers are able to devote more time to training a bird.

These falcons already know how to fly, but they do not associate food with people. To make the proper association with man and to guard against the vice of screaming, the weight of these falcons should be reduced gradually. A falcon with a healthy appetite will pay close attention to its lessons, and is unlikely to fly off chasing anything and everything, as would a fat and playful imprint. This business-like approach to training minimizes the likelihood that the falcon will be lost and reduces the time demanded of the falconer. These birds offer an alternative for the falconer who is not interested in raising and indulging an imprint for several months before its talents can be employed in the field.

The Traditional Hack

For centuries, falconers have taken young eyasses from their eyries and placed them in small sheds on stilts. The "hack

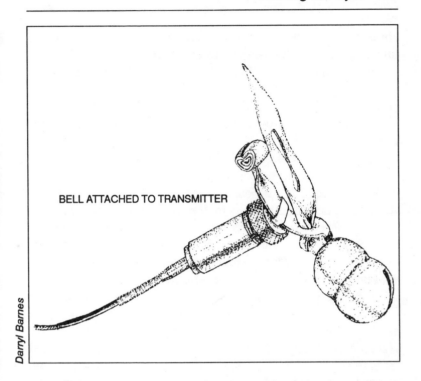

BELL ATTACHED TO TRANSMITTER

Darryl Barnes

hut" serves as a nursery and is off the ground to ensure that the quarters are inaccessible to ground-dwelling predators. Food is supplied for the eyasses through a slot, so that the birds do not associate feeding with people. As the eyasses develop, they are free to come and go as they please. But for several weeks after "fledging," the falcons are unable to hunt on their own so they return to the hack hut for food. Activities of the birds are observed closely. As soon as the falcons make a kill or fail to return to the hack hut at night, they are trapped and training begins.

At this stage, the eyas is 10- to 12-weeks old. It is strong and well-muscled but still young and impressionable. These falcons train quickly, as a rule, and do not display the bad habits associated with eyas birds, such as screaming and mantling. The advantage to a hacked eyas is that it has developed the physical condition and mental outlook of a wild falcon. The season starts about the time these birds are learning to take a pitch, so the falconer may proceed directly to game hawking.

In recent years, The Peregrine Fund has developed a hack-tower release method for reintroduction purposes that has great potential for use with falconry birds. Five-week-old eyasses are placed in a special release box equipped with a food chute and barred front. The eyasses are restrained inside the box until they are 42- to 45-days old. Then, the bars are removed and the falcons are liberated. But for falconry purposes, eyasses are fed from a board or other structure at which they will be trapped, traditionally by bow net, at the termination of the hack. To ensure their recovery, transmitters should be placed on these birds. Potential hack sites should be carefully scouted for avian predators (great horned owls and eagles) and territorial wild falcons that could endanger the young falcons.

Even more elaborate are the towers used to hack large falcons in the mountains of Saudi Arabia. These buildings serve as observation blinds as well as feeding and trapping stations. Hacking sites may take many forms. Falcons can be hacked from the tops of barns, silos, and freestanding scaffolding, anywhere that they are safe from aerial and mammalian predators.

7 Passage Prairie Falcon

My introduction to trapping prairie falcons came in the fall of 1969. Our destination, the high desert plains, was a 5-hour car trip from college. During the drive, we would cross a major mountain range, change climates, vegetation, and terrain, and arrive in the kind of place that most people associate with the Wild West.

Wes Pike, Allan Cline, and I had crammed ourselves, our bedrolls, and our trapping paraphernalia into a Volkswagen "Beetle" for the weekend trek. Leaving the rainy Willamette Valley, we descended from the crest of the Cascade Mountains into the dry, cold climate of the Basin and Range country. During the wee hours of the morning, we arrived in prime prairie falcon habitat. It was a remarkable experience. To this day, the impressions of a clear, moonlit sky, the crackling fire of pungent juniper wood, and the cold canopy of twinkling stars are haunting recollections of the adventures of youth.

The following day was almost overwhelming. We awoke to a crisp, clear sunrise amidst a stand of sweetly-scented pine that bordered a huge sagebrush basin. Around us, in the far distance, buttes and escarpments rose from the basin floor like benign giants. During the course of the day, we would make our drive-by introductions to the local black-tailed jack rabbits, sage grouse, coyotes, and mule deer. At one point, a herd of perhaps one hundred pronghorn antelope caused us welcome delay while they crossed the washboarded dirt road directly in front of the car. Their peculiar habit of racing toward a fence, then ducking under it at the last second, in preference to jumping the obstacle, was most amusing.

My previous attempt to trap a wild prairie falcon had been a dismal failure. In contrast, Wes had trapped and trained a number of these desert falcons. Because he knew both the birds and the country, I was hoping to learn a lot from him. Our timing for this trip was right. By early November, snows in the high country had forced the transient falcons down into the valley floors for the winter. Not only that, but it was cold, and ground squirrels, the major food item for prairie falcons during the summer, were underground. These conditions made for hungry falcons. As is typical of good trapping areas, we drove past a number of birds of prey while searching for prairies. Under ideal conditions, one may see dozens of red-tailed, rough-legged, and ferruginous hawks, kestrels, and golden eagles before locating a prairie falcon.

We saw a handful of falcons that day and trapped two using pigeon harnesses: custom-fitted leather jackets with slip-knot nooses, attached to a weighted drag line. The only formal reference to the use of the pigeon harness, in *North American Falconry and Hunting Hawks* by Beebe and Webster, strongly advocated this trap for capturing large falcons. In intervening years, however, I've found it to be an unsatisfactory means of capturing prairie falcons under most circumstances. While the pigeon harness works well in extremely open places like ploughed fields and sandy beaches, it becomes decidedly ineffective in areas of fences, sagebrush, and all forms of tall cover. After trapping falcons for both falconry and research purposes, it has been my experience that a dho-gazza net, baited with a starling, is the preferred method. Were I limited to a single trap for capturing all North American falcons, my first choice would unquestioningly be the dho-gazza. Considering the price of gasoline, and the limited opportunities one normally has for trapping falcons, I am inclined to go with a high-percentage technique.

Over the years, Wes and Allan taught me much more than a few tips on falconry and hawk trapping. I think what they imparted in me was a personal appreciation for the high desert and the unique role of the prairie falcon in it. Ultimately, nothing got me as connected with wild birds of prey as going to where they lived and studying them in their natural environment.

Through trapping, one is required to seek the falcon on mutual ground, locate and identify it from other birds of prey, and, finally, coax the predatory instincts that allow it to be caught. Many falconers find trapping a compelling and challenging pastime. Sometimes surprising, occasionally disappointing, every day spent trapping is both educational and different.

Under these kinds of field conditions, one may also glimpse the powers of flight that distinguish wild falcons from their trained counterparts.

Trapping, like hawking, is a sensory-rich experience. It's a search-and-learn process that yields practical information to the student of raptor behavior. From a falconer's perspective, this information is useful for adapting the general principles of falconry to the behavior and ability of the specific species of raptor. My observation is that, as a whole, falconers are more inclined to do things the other way around.

It is unfortunate that many of today's falconers have never trapped and trained a wild falcon larger than a kestrel. A singularly important facet of North American falconry, begun in 1939 when Alva Nye trapped the first tundra peregrine at Assateague Island, Virginia, was the trapping and training of wild falcons for use in our sport. This annual event was, in large part, responsible for the high level of falconry attained in North

America and is an indelible part of our occidental sporting heritage. I believe it is extremely important for falconers to perpetuate this legacy, to maintain the time-honored and unique set of skills that made us what we are, and to further advance this body of knowledge for those falconers yet to come.

For many falconers, the passage prairie falcon may be the ideal hunting partner. It is an excellent choice for those who value a bird's previous hunting experience above dependability in the field. When taken from the wild, the seasoned passage falcon is physically and mentally tough, fully conditioned, and thoroughly skilled in the techniques for killing game. Unlike the eyas, it has already faced a hostile environment and learned how to survive.

In effect, the falconer elects to accept questionable loyalty in return for the passager's proven hunting skills. The reality is that there is no inherent security in falconry at any level. One is simply cognizant of the tradeoffs and their implications. While the result is essentially the same, the approach for teaching a passage bird to perform as a game hawk differs in many respects from that used in training an eyas.

It is probably safe to say that the falconer who takes a passage prairie falcon from the wild will believe in love at first sight. However, the relationship between the falcon and the falconer will start out as a totally one-sided affair. At first, the passage bird will have every reason to be suspicious of the falconer and no reason whatsoever to cooperate. If one expects to enjoy more than a brief flirtation with this new partner, the falconer must gain the falcon's trust.

Prairie falcons can be caught with a variety of traps, including: pigeon harness, dho-gazza, pandam, and bal-chatri. The use and effectiveness of any trap are highly dependent on local conditions. Because trapping is an art form in and of itself and because there are a number of falconry articles and texts that cover the subject thoroughly, I advise the reader to study this subject through the available literature. The best way to learn is to have an experienced falconer demonstrate safe trapping techniques.

HANDLING THE FRESHLY-TRAPPED FALCON

Trapping a gorgeous passage falcon is a stellar event. There are few moments as exhilarating as running up to a freshly snared passage falcon and finding that the bird is *exactly* what you wanted. The coal black eyes are piercing and the sun-bleached plumage will never again be quite as beautiful as at that moment. However, the falconer must make every attempt to preserve the falcon in its pristine condition.

For centuries, falconers have known that the best way to restrain and transport a wild-trapped falcon is to place the bird in a sock and keep it hooded. A sheer nylon stocking with the toe removed works perfectly. Ordinary masking tape can be attached loosely on the outside of the sock to truss the falcon safely inside. Wide strips of masking tape can be wound around the falcon's crop area and then wrapped carefully to encircle the falcon's body just above the feet. Tape should also be used to keep the falcon's talons folded and closed. This will prevent the falcon from shredding the nylon stocking with its talons, and ensures that it will not accidentally puncture its own feet when struggling to escape. Hooding and socking minimize the effects of shock on the newly-trapped falcon. However, a socked falcon can overheat quickly, particularly during warm weather or

DHO-GAZZA NET
Darryl Barnes

when placed inside a heated car during winter. Experienced trappers recommend the absolute minimal use of the sock. Alva Nye told me that a bird should not be left in a stocking for more than one hour at a time, even if it means resocking the bird several times on the way home. It may become cramped and constipated, thus exaggerating the already stressful conditions of a traumatic capture. For a long trip home, the falcon may be carried hooded on the fist or placed on a car perch or cadge. Accommodations must be designed to prevent damage to the freshly trapped bird in transit.

During the early weeks of handling, the falcon's feathers will be most vulnerable to damage. To protect them, the tail should be bound with brown gum tape. Another effective measure to protect both the falcon and falconer from injury is to snip the sharp tips off the talons and the beak. This precautionary trimming, done at the time of capture when the decision is made to keep the bird, prevents the falcon from puncturing its feet during a wildly fluttering bate, and will save both the equipment and the falconer's fingers if the falcon is prone to bite or foot.

MANNING

Manning is the process whereby the falcon learns to acclimate to the sights and sounds around it. Manning is complete when the bird accepts its surroundings with passive indifference. A falcon is flown in relatively remote areas, but it often encounters people, animals, and machinery foreign to it. In order to suppress its instincts to flee from alarming situations, the falcon must be psychologically prepared. It is the manning process that provides this preparation through the home life and social exposure the falcon receives.

Here is a simplified scheme for manning a passage falcon, designed to minimize trauma to both the bird and its trainer. Ideally, the falconer will use a properly fitting hood from the outset and attempt to man the falcon with as few bates as possible. The hood is an indispensable item that reduces the shock of capture and eases the handling and transportation of the falcon. Wild falcons bite and scratch hoods, so use an old one for the first two weeks. Anglo-Indian hoods are the most practical at this stage, as they are easy to put on and will not overly inhibit a falcon that needs to cast. The critical time for casting occurs within the first twenty-four hours (often the next morning) after capture. For that reason, I prefer to leave a fresh falcon unhooded in a darkened room until the morning after capture. After that time, the trainer can control the intake of casting material to fit into the training schedule of the falcon. Initially, when not being handled, the hooded falcon should be kept in a darkened room and tied to a portable block on top of a padded floor. Some falconers arrange to have a radio playing during these periods so that the falcon is constantly hearing voices; this also tends to keep the birds awake longer than if they were left in absolute silence. If the falcon bates off this low perch, it will land on the padded floor. There is no danger that the bird will hang upside down as it would do on a screen perch. Should it manage to slip its hood while unattended, the falcon is likely to sit quietly in the darkened room rather than bate toward a window.

Control of passage prairie falcons is achieved largely through appetite and weight regulation. Because they are capable of prolonged fasts, the birds should not be overfed during training. A food whistle call or sound should be used from the beginning as a means for getting the falcon's attention and identifying its trainer. During feeding times, some falcons eat only half a crop of food, then begin to fidget and bate. Therefore, the falconer must constantly observe the attentiveness of the pupil. It is a simple matter to hood a fresh falcon that is intent on eating, and is advisable to leave the bird a bit hungry after each meal.

The first meal is often a stumbling block for both falcon and falconer. The falcon is gripped by fear of people and the strange surroundings. The falconer must use self-control, an economy of movement, and the proper presentation of food to entice it to eat. However, the sooner the falcon begins eating, the sooner it can advance in its education. Instead of feeding the falcon through the hood, curb the conditions that cause it to bate and encourage the falcon to feed bareheaded from the start. With the falcon already fearful, the fewer strange scenes to distract it from the business at hand, the better. To achieve the desired effect, the falconer should sit alone in a quiet room across from a low-wattage lamp. By using a dimmer switch, the falconer can vary the amount of light as needed. This method is preferable to the eerie, flickering candlelight suggested in some of the older falconry manuals. Prior to unhooding the falcon, the falconer must make the necessary preparations to feed the bird with minimum motion. The chair should be positioned a safe distance away from any obstacles that the falcon might accidentally hit while bating. An adequate supply of small pieces of meat (about the size of jelly beans) should be cut and placed within reach of the chair. A plucked pigeon breast makes a tempting offering and may be held in the gloved hand before the hood is gently removed from the falcon's head.

The falcon will usually bate, hiss, and vocalize to some extent upon being freed from the hood. This is likely to be the falcon's first opportunity to release its pent-up energy since capture. A few hearty bates, along with a mute or two, will leave no doubt that the falcon is a healthy specimen. At this point, the falcon should be held so that its chest is nearly level with the face of the falconer. Eye contact should be carefully avoided. The falconer's gaze should focus on the falcon's feet. All subsequent movements must be slow and deliberate. Even the slightest flinch of the falconer may trigger a bating frenzy. Eventually, the falcon will sit the fist. The bird will then stare and hiss whenever the falconer moves, but this is a step in the right direction.

After the falcon has regained its wind, the falconer may then move the plucked pigeon breast against the falcon's feet and tempt the falcon to take a bite. Occasionally, the falcon will bite the meat if it is held up near the crop. More often, the falconer must offer the falcon a taste of the meat to spark its interest in eating. The falcon will sometimes snap at a morsel of meat pressed against the side of its mouth where the mandibles join. It is extremely important that the falconer's hand not jerk back when this happens, even though the bird may bite in the process. Frightening the falcon at any time, especially at this crucial point, is self-defeating. Usually, the falcon will sit with the food in its mouth until the falconer gently pushes it into the back of the bird's throat, causing it to either flick the meat away or to swallow it. In either event, the piece must be followed by another offering until the falcon takes the food freely. After tasting a few small pieces of meat, some falcons will lean down and begin, shyly and cautiously, to pull at the pigeon breast. However, it may be necessary to tempt the falcon again with the pigeon breast held closer to the bird's crop and chest. Once the falcon starts to feed, the breast can be gradually lowered until the falcon is repeatedly leaning down and pulling meat from the glove. It is imperative that the falconer ceases all movement whenever the falcon initiates feeding.

As soon as the falcon begins pulling from the pigeon breast in earnest, the breast should be "palmed" so that the falcon must work on the bony portions instead of the attractive but quickly consumed muscle. Then the precut pieces of meat may be presented intermittently as the falcon pulls from the fist. Feeding a falcon from one's fingertips lays the groundwork for important training steps. Such feeding serves to overcome the bird's fear of a moving hand and encourages it to look to the falconer for tasty tidbits. Then, when the falcon is engrossed in eating or looking for food, it is often a simple matter to hood the bird. With finesse, this task may be performed in a manner that ends each lesson on a positive note.

A wild falcon that is not inclined to eat is capable of bating itself sick. Under these conditions, the falconer is forced to hood the bird and wait for a more congenial mood. Some freshly trapped prairie falcons have refused food for periods as long as a week. Because such stubbornness could ultimately weaken the falcon, every effort should be made to induce the wild falcon to eat as soon as possible. Most falconers first attempt to feed the falcon in the evening on the day following capture, after all casting material has been passed.

The trauma of trapping can cause a falcon to retain casting material for more than twenty-four hours. There is no way to know if a falcon ate or cast before it was trapped. Therefore, it must be watched closely and one should never assume that the bird can cast through the hood. A tight fitting hood can choke a falcon when it casts and, at the very least, casting material can make a mess of a finely crafted hood. For the first two weeks of training, I don't feed any casting material.

Manning is best accomplished while the falcon is engrossed in a meal and paying little attention to otherwise threatening sights and sounds. Thus, the falcon should be exposed to its new environment at a slow and controlled pace during feeding sessions. An upset falcon that bates at something new should be hooded and reintroduced to the experience at a greater distance the next time. The process should be repeated until its fear is overcome. Because birds of prey are generally restless at dusk and calmer after dark, evenings are an ideal time to handle a new bird. Falcons that are inclined to bate in daylight are often content to sit the fist or a perch at night. As the falcon adjusts to its surroundings, its "free time" periods can begin. The bird should be offered tidbits during these periods, and should be hooded occasionally. Some authors recommend repetitive hooding of a new falcon as a means of hood training, but some falcons resent such harassment. Hooding should not be overdone at any time. If the falcon takes the hood without a fuss, it is best to leave well enough alone.

Generally, 10 percent of the falcon's weight at the time of capture is dieted away. This weight is determined after the falcon has cast but before it has eaten its first meal in captivity. Electronic scales give the most accurate measurement of weight. Most scales can be modified to accommodate a perch for the bird. By recording the daily weight and behavior of the falcon, one will discover its operational weight range. The falcon should be kept in as robust or high a condition as possible. This aids the sound health of the bird and reduces the chance for behavioral anomalies, as a small percentage of passage prairie falcons are inclined to scream and mantle when genuinely hungry.

As the bird's weight is reduced, it begins to regard the falconer's approach with less fear, and then with expectation. During the first two weeks or so, the falcon should be left hooded on the portable block in a darkened room. After that, the bird may be left unhooded at night so that it may be fed casting material (feathers, bone, etc.) that will be disgorged in the early morning without the encumbrance of the hood. Gradually, as the falcon permits the falconer to approach and feed it on the inside block, more liberties may be taken. The bird may then be left unhooded during the day, introduced to the outside block, and tethered to higher perches for more formal training, if desired.

A falcon left unhooded on a block or perch for the first time will surely bate, but most falcons regain their perches with little hesitation. The falconer must then reach in periodically to the falcon and offer food without scaring the bird. If the falcon is secured to a high, indoor perch, such as a round perch or shelf perch, the falconer should have no problem approaching the falcon to offer it tidbits, but must always avoid staring at the falcon. On the other hand, approaching a jittery falcon on an outside block requires special care and considerable stealth. The falcon will no doubt perceive the human form as ominous. The falconer should approach at a leisurely stroll in a circuitous manner, culminating in a low crouch with an arm outstretched. By sounding the food whistle and shaking fingers with the food, the falcon's attention may be focused on the trainer. Tidbits should be presented by leaning in slowly and offering the morsel on the fingertips near the falcon's feet. In this way, the falcon does not become frightened by a hand coming at it from above, and the falconer is in less danger of being grabbed. While short-winged hawks strike at the meat with their talons, falcons generally do not. As soon as the falcon accepts the food, one should withdraw slowly. The falconer can then circle the block and continue tidbitting or offer the bird a larger piece of meat on the glove. It is unwise to attempt to hood a falcon that is standing on a block. Should the falcon bate, a wing beating against the block could easily damage its primaries.

Nearly every nonhunting activity in which one involves a falcon may be termed "manning." While it isn't essential that a falcon be well-tamed in order to hunt, the day-to-day handling of the bird and, ultimately, the falconer's attitude toward the bird are enhanced when the falcon is well-behaved. Even the impressionable imprint will require a certain amount of maintenance manning.

One of the fastest ways to man a wild falcon is by the age-old technique called waking. The falcon is carried night and day for two or three days after capture. During this time the bird is stroked, fed intermittently, and gradually becomes exhausted to the point where it accepts its strange, new world with some degree of composure. Realistically, the practice requires two or more people to handle the falcon in shifts. While this method is not required, it does have the effect of settling the falcon into its new routine much sooner than would otherwise be possible. A falcon is more inclined to accept strange scenes with minimal resistance when it is tired. The same scenes have less impact later when the falcon is no longer tired and sees them for the second time. To some extent, long automobile trips have a similar calming effect on a freshly-caught falcon.

PREFLIGHT TRAINING

As the passager becomes tamer and accustomed to the daily feeding schedule, it may be taught to jump to the fist for food. Unlike hawks, falcons need not fly long distances to the fist. Once the bird comes promptly to the fist from 30 or 40 feet, the lure should be introduced. This is easily accomplished by tying an attractive offering to a lure that is laid on the ground in front of the hungry falcon as it sits on a block. The falcon should be allowed to drop down to the lure and eat a reasonable amount before the falconer makes in. The falconer then coaxes the falcon to abandon the lure for an equally appealing offering held in the gloved fist. By attaching a small amount of food to the lure, one may encourage the passage falcon to come to the glove for the majority of its food. Each meal should end with the passage falcon safely secured and under the control of the falconer. Thereafter, the creance or safety line should be attached to the falcon during training sessions until the bird can be trusted to fly free.

As in all phases of falconry training, the initial yard work should be done in seclusion to ensure that the falcon learns its lessons without distractions. Calling a falcon to a lure two or three times a day is sufficient for training purposes.

Because carrying can be such a troublesome vice, anticarrying precautions should be undertaken while the falcon is being lure trained. All early stages of the falcon's handling and training are designed to win its trust and may be deemed an anticarrying technique. Anticarrying training is essentially an extension of the tidbitting practice under field conditions. It promotes a genuine bonding between the falcon and falconer and allows the falcon to be reclaimed in situations where the bird is capable of flying off with small quarry. As a result of this training, the falcon has no fear of being robbed of its food and remains stationary when approached on a kill. This training utilizes the same cautious approach as one would use when tidbitting a wild falcon for the first time. Throughout manning, lure training, entering, and hawking, the falconer should offer the falcon tidbits. This is especially important while the falcon eats on the ground. By slowly approaching the falcon in concentric circles, the falconer may make in to the bird in an unthreatening manner. Using this technique, even the wildest of falcons may be convinced of the falconer's good intentions. With the falcon on the ground, feeding off the lure, the falconer gradually walks obliquely closer and closer to the falcon, then reaches out and offers the bird a tidbit. The falconer retreats and repeats the process five or six times using the food call or whistle at each approach. These actions are designed to demonstrate the falconer's good will, and should be repeated often, both at home and in the field. Consistency on the part of the falconer may make the difference between a falcon that allows itself to be picked up during some unforeseen emergency and one that is lost forever.

Despite all reasonable precautions, some falcons seem prone to carrying. It has been my experience that neither sex of prairie falcon is capable of making off with a large pigeon (there may be exceptions), but the falconer should exercise caution when loosing a new falcon at game that might tempt it to carry. It is far safer to match the falcon to a quarry that will ground it. This prolongs the verdict of "carrier" or "noncarrier" until some accident or incident puts the falcon to the test. Although carrying may be annoying and inconvenient, it does not follow that all falcons that carry will be lost because of it. Falcons that have packed off a substantial meal may often be recovered later. If the falcon can be found before it has fed, it may return to the lure with the small bird in its foot. On several occasions, I have even recovered a fully gorged passage falcon by throwing out a tethered pigeon and crawling in to grab the jesses.

Once the falcon comes instantly to the lure from 100 yards away, a tethered bird, such as a pigeon, should be introduced. Curiously, some passage falcons will sit nonchalantly on a block as a tethered bird flutters enticingly only a few feet away. This is analogous to a short-winged hawk that becomes fist bound; its predatory nature is inexplicably suppressed as a result of its training. If the falcon is hungry, the trance will be broken quickly and the falcon will pounce on the pigeon. It is important to give the falcon a good feeding from this bird.

Hereafter, the falcon will respond quickly to the flick of a bird wing or carcass. Known as a "dead lure" in falconry jargon, the carcass is a convincing method for entreating a falcon to return to its earthbound comrade. Even more convincing is a tethered pigeon, which almost always triggers a desirable reaction in a falcon. The use of a tethered pigeon should be reserved for perilous moments when a sluggish response to the lure from the falcon might result in its loss or otherwise place the falcon's life in peril.

8 Waiting-on Training

Thirty years ago, very few North American falconers had ever caught wild game with a trained falcon. Today, our collective skills and abilities have been greatly enhanced through a free and open exchange of ideas; falconry publications and social functions facilitated by the North American Falconers Association and numerous local falconry organizations have helped spread the word and the way. My time in the sport tracks this maturation period. Many falconers, new and old, have benefitted from the ideas and techniques brought to light during this era.

Over the years, I have passed through different stages in my quest to master the art of game hawking. It has been my good fortune to meet competent falconers and see falcons flown at the full spectrum of suitable quarry. Styles of falconry, like flight characteristics of falcons, vary with individuals. The styles or methods of falconry that I applied were, therefore, a synthesis of what I read, saw, and learned. For the most part, I simply took ideas created by more fertile minds and applied them to my particular circumstances. I've been guided by the saying: Learn from the mistakes of others, you won't live long enough to make them all yourself!

For some, there comes a time when a single goal dictates the direction that their falconry will take. While my aspirations have always centered on the hawking of wild game with longwings, my specific goals have changed over the years. At one point, catching any type of quarry with any falcon in any style meant satisfaction. But today, I am focused on the flying of falcons from extremely high pitches at specific types of aerial quarry.

Fortunately, I live in a place with suitable quarry, open terrain, and cooperative weather for most of the year. The down side of this loose style involves its inherent restrictions and potential dangers. An essential element of this style of falconry is great open spaces without check. The word check, one of many coined by our English colleagues, describes any undesirable bird that distracts a falcon from its job. Even here in the West, avoiding check generally means driving long distances from home to isolated hawking tracts. The best time of day to encourage falcons to fly to extreme heights is early afternoon. This is when climatic conditions do most to assist the ascending falcon. These are conditions necessary to encourage a falcon to take a truly high pitch; one that, with luck and planning, won't be subverted by external distractions before game is produced.

For much of the hawking season, therefore, I spend an inordinate amount of time traveling to suitable hawking places. Generally, I arrive at a time of day when game is inactive or hard to find. The obvious drawback to hawking in these remote areas is that a lost falcon is difficult to recover. My only equalizer in this affair is radiotelemetry. As one might imagine, my hunting opportunities are limited to a window of proper flying time, generally 2- to 3- hours per day. By necessity, I fly less often, spend more time finding a slip, and am afforded proportionately fewer kills over the course of a season than might otherwise be available.

Why, you may ask, do I bother? Because I firmly believe that falcons have never been trained to fly better than they are right now. It is my opinion that, under a given set of circumstances, trained falcons can come as close as realistically possible to approximating the actions of wild falcons. This certainly holds true for prairie falcons that regularly hunt from a high, commanding pitch over great expanses of desert and plains. I have yet to see any natural scene as spectacular as a falcon stooping to earth from beyond the limits of vision. The authors of yesteryear could only imagine witnessing this natural phenomenon on a daily basis. But then, they didn't have telemetry, high-powered binoculars, or 4-wheel drive vehicles to help them recover wayward falcons when things went wrong. If one views the progression of falconry as a continuum through time, then modern falconers are most assuredly on the cutting edge of a new approach to the sport. Unlike the genteel game hawking of Europe, North American falconers add an aggressive, hard-edged style to their falconry. Falcon technology, coupled with an attitude of experimentation, now marks the opening of new avenues for the pursuit of falconry.

In classical western falconry, the falcon is trained to mount high, circle overhead and wait patiently for beaters or dogs to flush quarry. This traditional waiting-on flight remains the essential part of modern game hawking. Game hawks must master this maneuver, much as figure skaters must learn to perform certain compulsory exercises.

Waiting-on is falconry's greatest challenge. This is where the falconer's efforts to instill trust and confidence have the greatest payoff. Without question, the flying lessons at this stage of training will rigorously test the strength of the bond between man and bird. The falconer expects the game hawk to play by the rules and stay around until game can be produced. In return for its patience and cooperation, the game hawk expects the falconer to present quarry in a timely manner.

The outcome of each waiting-on session thus depends upon two key factors that the falconer can never control completely. The most skillful falconer may have difficulty in providing regular hunting opportunities for the falcon. And even the most obedient game hawk will not regard patience as a virtue for long!

Waiting-on Training

The objective of waiting-on training is the same for the tame-hacked eyas, the nonimprinted eyas, and the passage bird; the falcon must learn to fly above the falconer long enough to be served. Early lessons are designed to teach the bird to look for the falconer, and the falcon's pitch is of little concern. In later lessons, the falcon must be taught to return at greater heights and remain overhead for longer periods of time. The lure is employed as a training device throughout these lessons, and the falconer terminates each session by throwing it to the ground. Falcons possessing a natural propensity to fly will begin to circle the falconer for longer and longer periods of time, waiting for the lure to appear. Once it waits-on obediently, the falcon is ready to be introduced to wild game.

The training of a passage falcon or a nonimprinted eyas calls for a conservative approach, and the falconer needs to keep close watch on the trainee. Early lessons should be restricted to brief flights. The bird must be directed to the business at hand, and foolish or wayward behavior should not be tolerated. In contrast, a more relaxed and permissive approach can be taken with tame-hacked eyasses. The latter can be brought around gradually to obedient behavior as they mature and as hunting urges preempt their desire for play.

At the outset, a falcon should be allowed to remain in the air only long enough to learn its lesson. In deciding the length of a lesson, it is good practice to follow the principle that the falcon should always be rewarded at the highest point it is expected to attain.

At first, the bird may be airborne for less than thirty seconds before the lure is thrown to the ground. Another sound practice is to serve the falcon in the climb, when it is pumping hard into the wind and making upward progress. The falcon soon learns to head skyward and eventually spends more time mounting in order to gain and maintain height. In the beginning, the falconer must monitor the bird's progress to make sure that its own flying style is not being impeded.

Some falcons mount in tight circles overhead while others go off hundreds of yards and climb on their way back to the falconer. One must observe the falcon to determine its style and adapt the training regime accordingly. It is often a fine line between the progression of waiting-on flights and wayward behavior. The falconer must learn to differentiate between suppressing the natural propensities of the falcon, and applying controls to prevent its loss.

As progress continues, the falcon may be allowed to fly for longer and longer periods before being served. The intent is not to make the bird wait, *per se,* but rather to improve its physical conditioning. It will be reassuring to know that the falcon will be able to go the distance when pursuing game.

The trainee is likely to react to waiting-on lessons in any number of ways, especially during initial stages. After being released by the falconer, some birds take the opportunity to explore the local countryside, often at considerable distance from the falconer. Others perch on a nearby fencepost to see what happens next or sit on the ground in apparent confusion. The falconer should be mentally and emotionally prepared to deal with an always interesting variety of possible responses.

The ideal falcon stays close by, flying above the trainer, and works upwind until the lure is served. If the falcon sits, the trainer should wait for it to fly again before presenting the lure. The bird can be taught obedience and patience by simply concealing the lure for longer periods in successive training sessions. After initial training, the falcon should be served only when waiting-on. When the falcon has learned to circle overhead and come to the lure consistently, the falconer may begin hunting or serve bagged game as a reward for good performance. In season, it is possible to release the falcon over a dog on point or near a small pond with ducks and present an opportunity to make a kill without prior use of pigeons or bagged game.

A falcon may become distracted during training sessions and depart for parts unknown. On such occasions, the trainer uses the lure and whistle to recall the missing bird. If it responds, the falcon should be rewarded promptly by dropping the lure to the ground. It is not at all unusual for the bird to start back toward the falconer before the lure is swung or the whistle is blown. If the lure is kept concealed, the falcon may pass above the falconer who keeps walking upwind through the field. After the falcon completes one or two revolutions, the lure should be thrown to the ground. Obviously, the falconer should reward the bird promptly when it has returned after being lost.

It is my philosophy that under no circumstances should one ever stoop a falcon to the lure, especially if it has been good enough to come of its own accord. A number of old "peregrine men" will argue this point with me. I have friends who stoop peregrines to the lure after they have been waiting-on and even after catching quarry. It is plain truth that peregrines tolerate more contrived handling techniques than their cousins, the desert falcons; the latter being less forgiving of error and more easily offended. When dealing with the headstrong, often volatile, personality of desert falcons, I believe the greatest benefits come from conveying simple ideas. My observation is that the practice of lure stooping, more than any other factor, caused the misconception that prairie falcons (and other species) do not wait-on well.

LIVE TRAINING AIDS

Falcons, like people, learn from their mistakes as well as their successes. Also, like some people, some falcons appear to have no desire to learn until they can grasp the objective and become fully convinced that the effort is worth their while. For example, a falcon may seem unable to understand the procedure until it actually gets the chance to chase birds. This is the time to employ bagged game or homing pigeons. The same falcon that sat dumbly when the lure was withheld may be more than willing to pursue a released bird. In any event, trial-and-error teaching methods using live training aids offer an excellent means for reinforcing initial waiting-on lessons and handling unusual cases.

The trial-and-error method of waiting-on training involves the "carrot and stick" approach. Here, the falconer introduces homing pigeons and bagged game as substitutes for the lure when the falcon is served. Food is always the motivating factor, and the falconer controls the time and place of pigeon releases, depending on whether the pigeon served is intended to escape or be captured. In early lessons, the falcon's attention becomes more focused on the falconer as it learns to expect pigeons to appear regularly from that vicinity. As training progresses, the falconer delays the pigeon release in order to increase the duration of the flights. By pursuing swift homing pigeons, the falcon quickly gains a realistic appreciation for the tactical advantage of speed and height. As a reward for taking a higher pitch, the falcon may be served an easy pigeon to kill. Allowing it to take generous feedings from its first few kills is sure to provide the strong incentive for continued improvement. Given enough hit-or-miss practice flights, the falcon will soon learn the techniques needed to challenge the pigeons and make them strain to evade the stoops. During training sessions, the falconer should provide easy kills as a reward for quality flying. Poor quality chases or misses should be rewarded with cold meat from the lure. The falcon will perform better next time. I like to think that falcons work to earn the more palatable delicacies; at least, they appear to prefer warm food to cold.

The standard remedy for a falcon that refuses to fly overhead is to release a strong pigeon that it cannot catch. The objective is to have the pigeon take the falcon high into the sky on a futile tailchase in which the falcon gains some height before giving up. According to theory, the falcon will then return to the falconer at its new pitch, at which time the falconer rewards it with an easy pigeon. In actual practice, however, the falconer must often run long and hard to get under the falcon and serve the bagged game before the bird descends to look for the lure. While gasping for breath, one is apt to ponder the reversal of roles and wonder: "Just what is the point that the falcon is trying to make?" Nevertheless, it is only the result that matters.

Some falcons are stubborn, lazy, or slow to learn; they prefer sitting to flying. When faced with this problem, some falconers forget how to think. The common, and totally incorrect, response to this predicament is to release pigeons in hopes that the falcon will fly. With that approach, the falcon will eventually become trained to sit until pigeons appear and then, and only then, will it fly. A far better course of action is to do nothing until it is on the wing.

For the impatient, there is another way. One may briefly wave a pigeon or hold it on a short tether to tempt the falcon off the perch. The waved pigeon signals the falcon to return and promises that a slip is forthcoming. By necessity, this signal must always be followed by a bird being served for the falcon to chase. Even if the falcon isn't very high, game of some sort must be produced. If the falcon begins to wait-on obediently, it should then be served when in good position. But if the falcon comes in low, a fast pigeon may be served when it is out of position, to take the falcon up into the sky and make it work.

A similar trick is used to attract a falcon that has raked away or is waiting-on out of position. The falconer waves a hat, handkerchief or anything visible, and then produces a slip when the falcon responds. Just as in the above situation, one wants the falcon to maintain its pitch and return to position. Thus, swinging the lure would again be sending conflicting signals to the falcon.

I once had a passage prairie falcon that steadfastly refused to take a pitch. Out of desperation, I began to serve it strong homing pigeons at a duck pond. When the falcon finally gave up tailchasing the pigeon and drifted back overhead, I would flush the ducks. Eventually, this falcon began waiting-on well and killed a number of ducks. This example clearly shows that there are no "school solutions" for every problem in falconry. When it comes to training, the best advice I ever heard was: "Whatever works!"

After a falcon has been trained with single pigeons and bagged game, it should be flown at flocks. I find it convenient to carry up to six pigeons in a burlap sack; the birds are released by holding the sack upside down. Likewise, a game catapult can release numerous birds simultaneously. The falcon must learn to chase and kill with these multiple releases. Thereafter, caution must be exercised when releasing one pigeon at a time, especially with an eyas. Success on singles could spoil the falcon and impair its future hunting ability in the field, as the falcon will be forever waiting for a single to appear. If the falcon shows no hesitation on flocks, however, it can be flown on single pigeons regularly. Of course, the best method to prevent a game hawk from being spoiled is to take the bird hunting and expose it to real-life situations *as soon as* it waits-on properly.

PITCH AND HUNTING TACTICS

In the final phase of waiting-on training, it is time to present the falcon with actual hunting opportunities and enter it on wild game. As one might expect, there are several preferred methods.

Proponents of the traditional method of waiting-on training extoll the virtue of teaching a falcon the value of pitch through experience. In this method, the game hawk learns to regulate itself to the most practical hunting height by trial and error. From a high pitch, in excess of 500 feet, the bird may not have time to complete a successful attack before the quarry escapes into cover. From a pitch that is too low, the falcon is unable to develop sufficient speed to overtake an accelerating game bird and strike an effective, debilitating blow. Simply flying the bird on game allows it to find the best height for capturing quarry under actual field conditions. This traditional method offers significant advantages. The falcon learns the capabilities of its quarry, and begins to develop successful tactics.

For the falconer blessed with access to ground abounding with quarry, the entering of an eyas is no great chore, especially if extended seasons are permitted. The falcon is released when a young game bird has been located visually, pointed by a steady dog, or flushed and marked down. The falconer then attempts to set up an advantageous hunting situation. When conditions favor the eyas, the game bird is flushed for the falcon to pursue. Given enough opportunities, the falcon should eventually score. Flights against game birds of all ages provide important lessons for the budding hunter. The falcon learns to stay high enough over the dog and falconer in order to command the situation below and to have the necessary speed and momentum to overtake and attack a wild-flushed bird. After a series of successful flights, the pitch and style of the eyas should improve steadily, and its flying habits should become predictable. Over time, the falcon becomes skilled as the wild game birds mature and offer greater challenge. A similar pattern is observed in hunting waterfowl. Ducks flushed from small ponds may be caught by a callow eyas from a modest pitch, but the situation changes dramatically when the falcon is loosed over large bodies of water, where the game has the upper hand. In any case, the falconer should match the eyas to more challenging quarry as its confidence and ability improve.

Another school of thought advocates that falcons be trained to fly well first and then entered on game later. The approach calls for conditioning the falcon to respond to a highly predictable series of events, and requires extensive use of homing pigeons and bagged game in a tightly-controlled training environment. Birds are always served for the falcon at exactly the right moment in each flight. Through repetition and regular success, the falcon eventually learns to go quite high and wait for the inevitable flush.

There is no question that some falcons trained in this manner put on fabulous performances in the air. Some falconers tend to carry such training to extremes and they strive to exercise such total control that their flights lack any form of spontaneity. In my opinion, this approach eliminates the elements of surprise that make real-life hunting so unpredictable and exciting. On their home ground, these falcons may achieve high-quality game hawking. If properly entered, they will kill game in the classical style. Unfortunately, they must learn the ways of their quarry later in the season. The procedure may be drawn out so long that the young game birds are fully grown before the falcon actually has an opportunity to pursue them.

Having never been "falcon rich," I always have been inclined to take a conservative approach to flying falcons. Once the falcon is taking a pitch of 150 to 200 feet, I enter it on game and start hawking. The falcon gradually learns to fly higher and modify its pitch to suit the quarry and terrain. Through on-the-job training, the falcon starts to pick up the valuable skills that will make it an effective game hawk. I strive to keep a new bird in continuous visual contact and be in close proximity to the stoop when it occurs. After investing all the time and effort needed to get this far, it is disappointing to miss out on the best part of the show!

THERMALS AND SOARING

In learning to take a pitch, all falcons eventually reach a practical ceiling that they seldom try to exceed. If the falconer lives in open country and possesses a good set of nerves, the falcon can be encouraged to keep climbing into the wild blue yonder and to take even higher pitches. By giving the falcon enough latitude to wander into the heavens, it can probably be trained to fly to exceptional heights, in excess of 2,000 feet, and perform sensational stoops. To achieve such performance, however, the falconer must relax the usual controls and give the bird a free hand to learn on its own. Consequently, this practice can be extremely dangerous. The advantages of the sky-raking pitch must always be weighed against the potential loss of the falcon.

Training for soaring flights can commence after a falcon begins to wait-on obediently. The bird is taken out early in the day and encouraged to soar and wander. The process is started by allowing the falcon to break off from its customary overhead position and to meander away from the falconer. While the falcon is still in range, and when its pitch is judged to be adequate, the falconer attracts the bird's attention and serves an easy pigeon to reward its behavior. With repetition, the falcon learns to expect a kill when it flies in this manner. As training progresses, the falconer should increase the degree of difficulty of successive flights. Gradually, the falcon is allowed to wander off a mile or more and gain great heights before returning overhead. As the bird attains these higher pitches, it is able to command tremendous ground area. It is not uncommon for the falcon to stoop back toward the falconer and kill a pigeon high in the air.

One must also take advantage of natural lift conditions created by thermals and wind currents to encourage the falcon to mount. Open country adjacent to benches, hills, and mountainsides provides an ideal training ground for such lessons. Dark, plowed fields and areas where lift is created by solar heat, air turbulence, or wind deflection are also suitable. Congregations of red-tailed hawks and vultures soaring in an area often indicate good lift conditions. Here again, pigeons are the preferred bagged game used to control the falcon's behavior. For several reasons, this training also entails significant risks. In the first place, the bird is flown at a higher-than-normal weight to encourage it to wander in the sky. In addition, this training is typically done at midday when conditions are ripe for a falcon to take off, climb into the blue, and just keep going! Nevertheless, with the back up offered by telemetry, the falcon may be encouraged to achieve greater heights and ranges than would otherwise be prudent. After a time, the bird may come floating back, a mere dot in the falconer's binoculars, anticipating the appearance of birds to chase. This is the time to reward the falcon's performance by releasing an easy pigeon. Often the falcon will be heard before it can be seen. In open country, the pigeon will have virtually no chance to escape the blistering attack, and the kill will reinforce the falcon's behavior.

During such flying lessons, the falcon is often on the wing for one to two hours. If the falcon becomes playful for too long a time, strong pigeons may be released to attract its attention. If off at a distance, the falcon may attempt a stoop, but the pigeon is generally too fast and too high to be in much danger. Waving a hat or glove prior to releasing the pigeon is often sufficient to bring the falcon into position overhead. The falcon soon learns to associate the waving object with a flush and responds correctly.

Once the falcon learns to look for lift, it will seek out thermals or power up into the sky looking for wind currents.

Falcons that occasionally putter around at a low pitch may be discouraged by releasing a good homing pigeon that cannot be caught. The miss may prompt the falcon to seek lift in order to get higher and dominate the game. After attaining the desired height, the falcon will then come back into position where it can be served an easy pigeon as a reward. This soon becomes a spectacular game: the falcon heads toward the clouds and returns overhead to be served small flocks of released homing pigeons. The homers simulate flocks of game birds and are used to accustom the falcon to the confusion of a multiple flush.

Special care must always be shown in starting out eyasses with this method. They are so untrustworthy and unpredictable that there is substantial risk of loss. With a fat imprint, the falconer cannot exert the appetite control measures so immediately useful with nonimprinted falcons. The behavior of an imprint is guided more by conditioning factors such as the daily flying schedule and its social interactions with people. While not quantifiable, these are powerful motivators. Even reliable birds will need some pang of hunger to keep them playing the game. Training an eyas to take a spectacular pitch may or may not be appropriate, depending on the type of terrain, weather, and game in the hawking area. They can always be taught to fly thermals after they have been through a season. I know of several eyasses, and passage falcons, that learned to fly thermals later in life. In the case of first-year eyasses, their pitch may be more susceptible to the negative influences of changing weather patterns as compared with wild-caught falcons that have faced inclement weather before. Poor footing ability, a characteristic of eyas falcons in general, can be greatly exaggerated under these circumstances. In the early stages of training, eyasses lack the good sense and caution of their wild counterparts. More than one promising young falcon has been caught and killed by a golden eagle while under the intoxicating influence of high-altitude flight. Furthermore, the playful and naively aggressive nature of many eyasses prompts them to attack larger raptors that occasionally turn the tables on them. A wayward eyas that suddenly feels like migrating, or a panic-stricken youngster trying to put distance between itself and a hungry eagle, is fully capable of flying hundreds of miles in a matter of hours.

Once trained, a falcon must be flown regularly to maintain its special flying style, but flights at game are often difficult to arrange. Unlike pigeons, most game birds won't stay in the air for long with the threat of a raptor overhead, and their tactics can frustrate a falcon. However, desert duck hawking and flights on prairie grouse and partridge in sparse, open country can keep a falcon flying high all season. Otherwise, the falcon too often sees its quarry escaping into cover while it is still descending from great heights. This experience results in a rapid deterioration of its pitch. It is necessary to vary flights at different kinds of game or to intersperse flights at topnotch pigeons over the course of the season in order to maintain the highest caliber of game hawking.

Weather patterns may alter a falcon's pitch; clear, dry weather is needed throughout most of the hawking season. Falcons that have learned to soar during summer and fall may become disoriented when winter weather patterns arrive. In the coastal northwest of North America, the thermals are gone by late October and the falcon must fly under its own power again.

After completing a molt, intermewed falcons may be encouraged to soar while building flight condition. Experienced game hawks that go through this warmup exercise prior to the hunting season can provide sensational early-season flights on game. Some of these falcons become specialized hunters and mount so high that the quarry can be hundreds of yards away from a flush before they finally get down for the strike. Furthermore, the loftier the pitch, the less likely that the falconer will be able to observe the entire flight-and-kill sequence. It is probably fair to say that a falcon so trained will not be an adaptable performer in every environment. This kind of falcon may be completely ineffective and useless to any falconer who does not have regular access to wide-open spaces. More than likely, only a few falconers live and hawk in country where such special training is advantageous.

Haggard prairie falcon taking a close look. *Rick Kline*

Until one has seen a falcon vaporize into the clear, blue sky and come down to kill flushed game, it is impossible to appreciate the advantages of a thermal pitch. In many respects, the attainment of a really high pitch adds a new dimension to classical game hawking. Unlike standard game hawking procedure, the falcon need not be directly overhead when game is flushed; it is often more exciting to spring game when the falcon is high and wide, permitting the quarry to reach top speed and be fully committed to leave before the falcon comes into view. When the falcon is not immediately visible, game birds will bypass scanty cover to fly long distances before putting in. Sometimes, it appears that the quarry isn't aware of the falcon until the last seconds before impact, making successful evasive maneuvers extremely difficult. Not only is this great spectator sport, but a falcon that is willing to wait-on for long periods of time permits one the luxury of hawking upland game on speculation with wide ranging pointers; quarry that might otherwise be difficult to pin down and flush at the appropriate time.

Unfortunately, thermal hawking is an artificial situation. Whether falcons can be relied upon to fly consistently in this manner for more than a few seasons has yet to be determined. Some falcons will do so only when warm thermals are available. Thus, falcons must be flown under extremely rigid conditions in order to perpetuate this unique style that is so spectacular.

9 Telemetry

In the days before telemetry, some of the better trained falcons would often chase and kill game out of sight or simply go off self-hunting and subsequently become lost. Falconers often commented that "you always lose the good birds." But today, we are fortunate to have the technology that permits us to retrieve such star performers.

It is far better to train and fly falcons properly than learn how to track down an absent game hawk. A high degree of self-discipline is required on the part of the falconer to refuse slips in potentially dangerous surroundings. When repeatedly offered poor slips, a falcon will abandon the falconer in search of better opportunities. An experienced falconer knows to recall the falcon before the hunting situation deteriorates. The more control a falconer exercises over the flight, the safer and more enjoyable it will be.

A young game hawk should never be rushed into a hunting situation until it is properly trained. Nor should an inexperienced bird be released in high winds, rain storms, and the like; it is almost impossible for young falcons to maintain pitch and position during inclement weather. Game should be solidly pointed or marked before the falcon is loosed, and each ensuing flush should be timed to give the falcon maximum advantage. A poor flush with the falcon out of position may result in a tailchase that takes the falcon out of sight. As well, the falcon should have a sufficient appetite to motivate it to hunt with the falconer. Zeal for a kill should never outweigh the falconer's desire to bring the falcon home safely.

Despite careful handling and training, even the best of falconers sometimes lose their game hawks. This happens most often when a falcon kills out of sight of the falconer. An unobserved kill may present a falcon with the opportunity to eat its fill and thus lose all incentive to return in search of the falconer. Trained raptors are occasionally lost for other reasons as well. In some instances, birds have been known to fly off with small quarry or simply rake away (i.e., stray) without any apparent provocation. In other cases, falcons have been frightened away or distracted by strange sounds or threatening situations. All too many falconers live in suburban areas and must, by necessity, fly their birds in marginal hawking terrain where such distractions are common.

The loss of a game hawk, even for a brief interval, is invariably a worrisome, trying experience! Having become totally dependent upon the falconer for its care and protection, an untrained eyas may not be able to survive for an extended period on its own. While lost, the bird could be exposed to any number of potentially harmful encounters. Malicious gunners, cats, dogs, eagles, owls, and a general public with little appreciation for birds of prey are constant threats to trained raptors. Depending upon how long the bird remains missing, the falconer's reaction will range from frustration and mild anxiety to genuine despair.

Fortunately for the falconry community, advances in microelectronics technology have produced an extremely practical and effective method for finding lost game hawks. Through the use of a radiotelemetry system, it is possible to track and locate a wayward bird over distances of twenty miles or more. The prime component of the system is the miniaturized radio transmitter that is attached to the falcon before it is released for a flight. Other essential components include a receiver and a directional antenna. These are available at reasonable cost and are quite reliable.

The equipment has no magical qualities that might induce the falcon to return to its trainer, but it does function as a superb tracking aid. I used radiotelemetry extensively to study the hunting and dispersal activity of wild prairie falcons, and became convinced of its indispensable value as a device for retrieving trained birds. In my opinion, such a system is as necessary to the modern falconer as a hood, leash, or a block. Given the present conditions for hawking in North America, any falconer who flies a trained game hawk without using a radiotelemetry system is knowingly courting disaster.

RADIOTELEMETRY EQUIPMENT

Transmitters are packaged as very small, lightweight units. Each transmitter is tuned to a specific frequency corresponding to one of several designated channels. When power is applied, the transmitter emits a continuous series of pulsed signals or "beeps" on its own preset channel, thus enabling each one to be easily identified. Two types of transmitter units are currently available: One type requires the insertion of a small hearing aid battery before the unit will operate. The other type has a self-contained battery with an external magnetic on/off switch or similar control. Both types have been extensively field tested and provide reliable performance. Personally, I prefer the units that operate on hearing aid batteries because they are smaller, lighter, and offer more flexibility in attachment.

Portable receivers are used in conjunction with a hand-held directional yagi antenna to detect and monitor signals. Receivers can operate on multiple channels by rotating a channel selector switch. Most receivers provide a meter to display the amplitude of pulsed signals. Headphones can be plugged in to monitor audio strength, and their use is strongly recommended. The signal will be strongest when the yagi antenna is pointed directly at the transmitter. Regardless of which channel is used, the reception range will be limited to strictly line-of-sight operation. Several different types of portable receivers are available commercially. Some are small, hand-held units that are easily

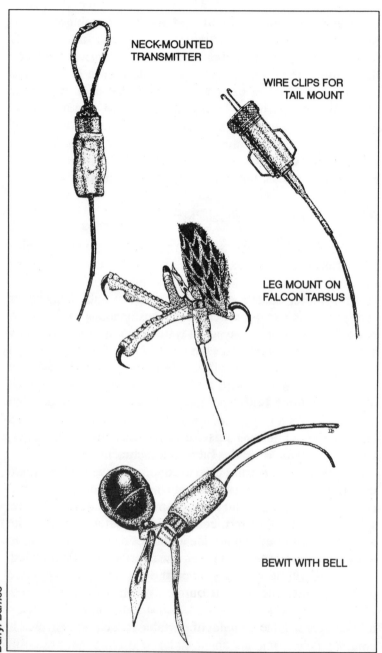

carried in the field on a belt holster. Larger units require a satchel with a shoulder strap to free the falconer's hands for holding the antenna, adjusting the receiver dials, and using binoculars.

There are a number of accessories that can enhance the basic telemetry system. Headphones and an omnidirectional, cartop antenna are desirable, inexpensive "options." Items that I have found to be most useful and convenient include: a battery tester, a quiver for carrying the folded-down antenna, spare batteries, antennas, bewits, antenna cable, electrical tape for field repairs, and aluminum foil for shimming up those few odd-sized batteries. Such extras should be kept handy for the day that Mr. Murphy joins you unexpectedly in the field.

ATTACHING THE TRANSMITTER

Electronics are not infallible. A number of falconers now play it safe and use two transmitters simultaneously on raptors large enough to carry them. Several alternative methods have been developed for attaching a transmitter unit to a game hawk. Leg-mounts, neck-mounts, and tail-mounts have all been successfully employed. Each of these methods has its pros and cons, as described below:

* Leg-mounts—With this method, the transmitter is fastened above the jess on the falcon's leg with a leather strap called a bewit. A variation is to attach the unit with a cable tie through the grommet in the Aylmeri bracelet. Of all methods, the transmitter is least likely to separate from the bird with a leg-mount. Small bells can be attached to the bewit as well, combining the equipment on one strap. Leg-mounts may not emit a clear signal when a falcon is sitting on the ground and may be difficult to attach to a falcon that is fidgeting and anxious to fly. Some hardhitting falcons may break the crystal in the transmitter. This happens rarely, and some manufacturers now offer shockproof crystals.

* **Neck-mounts**—Neck-mounts use a rubber band to hold the transmitter around the falcon's neck. A properly fitted unit will hold the transmitter just under the feathers on the falcon's crop. This method has the following advantages: the unit is easy to attach, the transmitter is not subjected to the shock of a falcon striking quarry, and it emits a relatively clear signal when the falcon is sitting or eating on the ground. The greatest drawback is the ease with which the transmitter can be accidentally removed, particularly if the falcon has pursued quarry into brush.
* **Tail-mounts**—A number of ingenious devices have been concocted to keep the transmitter attached to a falcon's tail feather. However, most falconers use a solderless electrical connector that is split down the barrel, glued, and crimped on one of the two decks or center tail feathers. Small alligator clips, soldered to the top of the transmitter, snap through the "eye" of the solderless connector to hold the unit in place. The more dependable "French clip" design uses two steel wires attached to the top of the transmitter, each with a small hook at the end. To mount the transmitter, the wires are pinched together and pushed into a catch device attached to a tail feather; outward pressure and the hooked ends hold the transmitter in place. However, clips are not foolproof and units have fallen off, been preened off, or knocked off by falcons that struck

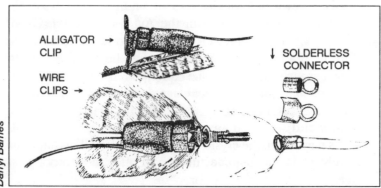

game hard. Cable ties may be used instead of the clip to ensure a more secure coupling. This system is convenient to use and has the advantage of elevating the transmitter somewhat to allow clearer signals when the bird is on the ground. However, some birds have been known to pull out the tail feathers to dislodge the transmitter. Damaged follicles can result.

TRANSMITTER CONDITIONING OF GAME HAWKS

Regardless of which attachment method is selected, the falcon must be thoroughly conditioned to accept and carry the transmitter. When exposing an eyas to a neck-mounted transmitter, the falconer should attach a dummy unit with a short antenna to the youngster's neck as soon as the bird is large enough to wear it. It has been my experience that any falcon that has learned to wear bells will ignore a leg-mounted transmitter. But purely for conditioning, a falcon may be left with the transmitter attached until it learns to ignore it. Many falcons will become nonchalant about transmitters after they have worn them for only a few hours. After the transmitter has been attached for several weeks, its presence becomes second nature to the bird. In fact, large birds such as gyrfalcons may even preen a neck-mounted unit so that it disappears beneath the feathers.

Unfortunately, not all falcons will tolerate certain methods for attaching transmitter units. I have had passage prairie falcons and gyrfalcons that consistently removed neck-mounted transmitters as soon as they were applied. However, these same birds totally ignored leg-mounted and tail-mounted units. Whereas most imprints may be conditioned to accept any attachment method, it may sometimes be necessary to experiment in order to find an attachment method that fits the personality of a particular bird.

Some falconers advocate leaving a neck-mounted unit on the falcon continuously, even during the molt. While this practice may not be necessary for many birds, such continuous acclimation has its advantages. Some care should be taken to cut the antenna very short on dummy transmitters attached to falcons that are tied to a block. Long antennas have been known to cause problems with tethered falcons by tangling in the jesses.

TRACKING

For practical purposes, maximum signal reception range always depends upon the differences in height between the transmitter and the receiving antenna. Uneven terrains, especially large features like mountains and deep canyons, become significant obstacles between the transmitter and receiver that can mask the transmitter, obscure the line of sight, and block out the signal completely. Such features may even cause signal "bounce," which makes the job of locating a bird much more difficult.

Assuming a clear and unobstructed line of sight, a rough rule of thumb can be used for estimating the maximum range of the tracking system. The range in miles is approximately equal to the square root of the height difference measured in feet. For example, if a falcon with a transmitter is flying over open country at a height of 100 feet, a falconer on the ground should be able to track the bird out to a distance of about ten miles. On the other hand, if that same falcon is feeding on perfectly level ground after making a kill, the falconer must search with the yagi antenna at least four feet high in order to detect a signal at two miles.

As suggested, height advantage is always a critically important factor in operating telemetry equipment. Terrain features and other obstacles present the falconer with adverse tracking conditions. One of the most frustrating situations occurs when a falcon makes a kill at the bottom of a gully, in a ditch, or in deep snow or water. Such difficulties can often be overcome simply by gaining a height advantage. Trees, water towers, barns, hill tops, and buttes can all serve as handy "elevators" to lift a falconer out of a blind spot. But steer clear of power poles and transmission towers! Not only can power poles be lethal to birds and people, but the static they create will drown out the transmitter signal.

When operating the receiver, it is important to keep the volume or "gain" turned down as low as possible. Changes in the strength of the "beep" signal will then be easier to detect, and the strongest return will be readily recognized when the yagi antenna is pointed directly at the falcon. For greater accuracy, the gain should be reduced as the falconer approaches the signal source. As the receiver gets very close to the transmitter, the signal becomes so strong that it appears to be coming from all directions. This is a common effect when trying to locate a falcon that is on the ground eating a kill in thick cover. By simply removing the antenna and pointing the coaxial cable or face of the receiver in the direction of the strongest signal, the falcon can usually be located. Small directional hoop antennas are very accurate at short range.

One must take numerous telemetric readings to locate a falcon that is lost, especially if it's on the move. The signal from a falcon that is leaving the country will come only from one direction. But the signal from a falcon that is sitting several miles away may vary in amplitude because the relative positions of the transmitter and receiver change. Therefore, it is important to triangulate to ensure that one is not passing by the falcon when it is stationary. For instance, if the falconer suspects that a bird has landed in a particular field, it would be necessary to take readings from at least two different sides of the field to know for certain if the falcon is there. A falconer can't afford to waste time walking through fields when a falcon might still be on the move straight ahead. When a falcon is soaring, the "beep" will be intermittently strong and weak, but always coming from one direction in a leisurely cadence. Similarly, a falcon may fly in an undulating fashion in strong winds, causing sporadic signal strength.

In the event that a lost falcon cannot be located by ground tracking, a light aircraft should be considered as a possible search vehicle. The aircraft will provide several hundred feet of height advantage, along with good speed for rapid area coverage. For expediency, the person tracking the bird from the air should communicate the falcon's position to someone in a chase car via two-way radio. Telemetry equipment is easy to install on an airplane. For best results, a pair of yagi antennas should be mounted on the plane, oriented to points ninety degrees on either side of the centerline. Each yagi can be connected by coaxial cable to the receiver in the cockpit, and a switch box should be added to select antennas. This arrangement will allow the receiver operator to monitor 360 degrees while the aircraft conducts a systematic search for the missing falcon.

OTHER SEARCH METHODS

There can be little doubt that the application of telemetry to game hawking is an important breakthrough for the falconry community. Nevertheless, no system is perfect. Even with the best telemetry, there always will be the possibility that a trained bird will be lost. Consequently, other search methods may be needed as backup.

We know from past sightings and recoveries that lost falcons may put hundreds of miles between them and their trainers in a matter of days. Based on my own experience, however, I strongly recommend that the falconer check back often at the place where the flight began. For some reason, many birds return to that place, particularly during the first few days following their departure. It may be possible to attract the truant from a great distance by swinging the lure and lofting pigeons. The range of visibility is undoubtedly the most important factor for all parties involved in the search, including the A.W.O.L. game hawk. I always attempt to find the highest ground with the best visibility so that the falcon may see me from any direction.

Knowledge of the homing instincts of eyas falcons may be of great benefit. These instincts were described by Ronald Stevens in his classic work, *Observations On Modern Falconry*. My own eyas falcons have homed to the hacking area. As long

Peregrine tiercel scratching an itch. *Rick Kline*

as the area is relatively safe, it may be comforting to know that the falcon is looking for familiar ground while it is on an unscheduled jaunt.

In planning a search, as suggested above, the place where the last flight began should be selected as the starting point. If the falcon cannot be located in the immediate vicinity, it will be necessary to search a wider area. All familiar hawking grounds within a 20-mile radius of the starting point should be thoroughly examined. Birds of prey, young eyas falcons in particular, are prone to fly in the direction of the prevailing wind. However, falcons can as easily fly in circles as go straight. Only intimate knowledge of an individual falcon's tendencies will help the falconer to anticipate its actions. Falcons are also good at finding places where birds congregate, like farms, feedlots, and marshes. This knowledge can be used to aid the search effort. Time can be a critical element, and delays may cause the search area to be enlarged. If friends with other telemetry units are available to assist in finding the bird, more thorough and rapid coverage is possible. By stationing one person at the starting point while others work systematically outward, the chances for success are substantially increased.

Whenever a falconer doubts the near-term prospects for recovering a bird, help should be sought from local residents and anyone else who can be mustered. Some radio and television stations in the area may be willing to assist by announcing a "missing bird" report in the form of a public service message. A newspaper advertisement with a picture of the falcon will get people's attention. Along with a possible crank call or two, the falconer is likely to receive some positive responses with valuable information, especially if a reward is offered for the safe return of the falcon. So long as the falcon's whereabouts and well-being remain in doubt, a dedicated falconer must seek assistance from all possible sources.

10 Falconry Dogs

A good dog is the greatest ally any falconer can have, and it is an indispensable member of any classical game-hawking team. True mastery of the sport entails orchestrating a falcon and dog to perform together in the field. Those who pursue the sport without a dog have missed the essential element of game hawking and a genuine sporting experience.

An obedient hunting dog will earn its keep in many ways. Anyone who has taken the time and effort to train a reliable gun dog will surely testify to the remarkable improvement in the quality of the sporting experience. Shooters have found that a single dog can often provide them with a tenfold increase in the numbers of game birds found and brought to bag during an outing. A well-trained dog will likewise enhance the quality of the falconry experience and frequently will produce even greater improvements. Not only is it far superior to beaters when hunting upland game, but a good dog will not hesitate to swim deep, cold water to pursue ducks.

Modern falconers choose from a number of different breeds for hunting, including spaniels, pointers, retrievers, and just plain mutts. Just about any hardy pooch with a good nose can be used with a falcon, provided it is obedient. The dog should be a good companion with plenty of "heart" and drive in the field. It must also mind commands and work close enough, or be trained well enough, to be controlled. Ideally, the first-class falconry dog will be easy to train. Whether this dog is versatile enough to hunt a variety of quarry or a specialist will depend on the needs and preferences of the falconer.

For regular success in hunting the upland game species, the falconer will need a dog that holds a steady point. A medium-range breed of the Continental stocks is always a practical choice. My personal preference is the Brittany Spaniel, the only pointing spaniel, due to its biddable nature, compact size, and intelligence. The German Shorthair, Wirehaired Pointer, Munsterlander, and Visla are also fine choices. It is a good idea to select dogs from pure hunting lines and avoid the show dogs. For this type of hawking, the dog must be trained to remain within a reasonable distance of the falconer, point and flush on command, and work well in water when the need arises.

The duck hawker who occasionally flies marked birds like quail or pheasants might consider a Springer Spaniel. Of the dogs bred originally for falconry, I believe that the Springer is the most overlooked. Springers make lovable companions and are excellent water dogs. They are trained to quarter directly ahead of the falconer, operating like a windshield wiper to flush game at close range. In heavy brush, their small size and short coat make them superior to retrievers. Considering the way modern pheasants tend to run rather than fly, Springers are as good as any breed at putting pheasants up in a reasonable amount of time. In classical game hawking, Springers played the subordinate role of "flusher" for quarry that had been located by a pointer.

For hunting widely scattered game in open country, the best choice is a long-gaited English Pointer or one of the setter breeds. These dogs are capable of covering huge acreage in short periods of time, serving best on birds that hold well to a point. I asked a respected dog trainer the difference between a good shooting dog and a good field trial dog. He said, "about a thousand yards." Dogs that run big and hold a staunch point are valuable for finding flights at upland game on expansive tracts of public rangeland. However, a falconer must cautiously consider these breeds because the field trial fraternity has bred

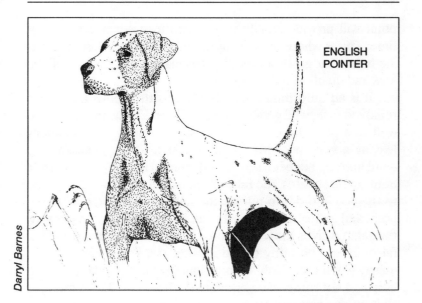

ENGLISH POINTER

Darryl Barnes

many lines of pointers and setters to run too wide for practical hunting on foot. These breeds are notoriously difficult to train and control; they are often hard to find or get lost when they make game out of sight of the hawking party. On balance, such breeds are likely to be of questionable value to the novice falconer or inexperienced dog trainer.

I advise any falconer interested in training dogs to begin working with one of the easier breeds and avoid unnecessary complications until one's techniques have been fully developed. Teaching a hunting dog to quarter close can be the most difficult part of the training process, but it is a lesson that is always important. A dog that is initially trained to quarter within gun range can later be allowed to increase the distance of its cast for more open country situations. Continental breeds are considered easier to train than English Pointers and setters, and they can be taught later to run wide if that is desired.

Like gunners, most falconers maximize their chances of success by hunting in areas known to hold significant numbers of game birds. A "high rolling" dog is not essential for locating game in such places. Any dog with a good nose and staunch point will provide quality slips within a reasonable period of time. This is where the lessons in obedience and close quartering have their greatest payoffs, particularly when hunting pheasants and quail.

It is an unfortunate fact that tight-sitting birds have been removed from wild game-bird populations. Birds that would lie well to a point have been systematically killed off, eventually leaving a gene pool for "runners." As a result, pheasant and quail hunting has been seriously degraded in many areas. While hunting these birds, the falconer must attempt to remain close to the dog in order to release the falcon immediately after the point and to flush as soon as the falcon is in position. In this way, the game is given the least amount of time to slink away, and the falconer can be fairly confident that the dog is close to the quarry when the "flush" command is given. A good dog should hold and not chase when birds are flushed. This allows multiple slips on one covey of birds.

For my style of hawking, I prefer to train a dog to drop (i.e., lie down) on command. To this end, I adopted the use of the voice command "hup" from the Springer Spaniel trainers. It is short, simple, and easy to call out, even when I'm out of breath after running hard. A hand signal is also useful, especially when a voice command might cause game to flush. The dog is first taught to respond to "hup," and the hand is raised in conjunction with the voice command. With repetition, the dog learns to recognize the hand signal and responds without hearing the verbal command. There may be times when the dog sees the hand signal and just keeps on going, but it should respond if the falconer adds the voice command. Hand signals can be also used to prevent a dog from overrunning a marked bird or causing a brace mate to break point. Ideally, a good dog should honor the point of a brace mate, but hand signals may salvage a slip when the dog forgets its manners. Being able to stop a dog with a raised hand is always a great convenience, and practice sessions may be held anywhere.

Although falcons occasionally kill directly in front of the falconer, more often the quarry is knocked down or chased into cover. When this occurs, the whole show starts over again, and the falcon must be waiting-on well before the field may move in for a reflush. Whether pursuing ducks or upland game, the falconer must keep the dog from preempting the planned follow-up actions. Being able to drop the dog at will can prevent an untimely flush by an overanxious pup caught up in the heat of the chase. This practice may also give the quarry enough sense of security, even if momentary, to hold in cover until the hawking party has reassembled and synchronized for the next attack. Any time gained allows the falcon to improve its position and may mean the difference between a successful kill and a fruitless workout. An obedient dog that is responsive to the falconer's control thus brings an added dimension and "esprit de corps" to field hawking.

It may help to have a dog that "foot scents" rather than "wind scents," especially when hawking in open, windy country. Some dogs will point birds from great distances by wind scenting. While that ability is often quite acceptable, it sometimes can cause problems for a falconer because one doesn't know exactly when a game bird will fly. The field may make several unsuccessful attempts to flush an expected quarry, only to find the dog creeping forward and "locking up" on point again further down the line. Such situations add to the normal difficulty of keeping an eye on the dog while watching the falcon to make sure that it is in good position overhead. It thus may become impossible to get around and head the quarry for a downwind flush, which is usually more advantageous for the falcon. Unless the falconer can stay right behind the dog and work up to the spot where the birds are lying, one is apt to bump the quarry prematurely.

A similar situation arises when the quarry runs ahead of the dog. Once the falcon is slightly upwind of the point, the falconer needs to rush in for the flush. In the event that the game has gone, one must watch the falcon to keep it overhead and encourage the dog to continue looking at a controlled pace. A dog that rushes ahead and bumps the birds will spoil the day; and a falcon that drifts out of position will give the game opportunity to depart. The falconer should stop all forward motion when the falcon is out of position and move briskly upwind behind the dog when the falcon is back in position. Eventually, the falconer will catch up to the quarry for the flush.

Some falconers believe that falconry dogs should not be trained to retrieve. I disagree. Loud reprimands are sufficient to teach most dogs not to bother a hawk. Falcons lack a game scent, and most bird dogs are not particularly interested in them. No trained hawking dog will retrieve a falcon, but it is amazing how often a downed game bird may be recovered by a hard charging dog. In hawking waterfowl, nothing takes the place of a dog that retrieves well, especially when a duck is hit over water and is unable or unwilling to take to the air. In such a situation, no one appreciates seeing that duck again more than the falcon!

Shooting over a dog is a great way to train it for falconry. In this way, the dog can be exposed to many birds under controlled conditions while the trainer concentrates on the dog's performance. Too often, falconers are so preoccupied with the actions of the falcon that they hurry their dogs, misinterpret their actions, or miss the opportunity to properly instruct and discipline a dog. As it is, most dogs don't see nearly enough birds during the course of the season. Any excuse to give them more field time is valid. Just as a trained falcon will perform well on a variety of quarry, a trained dog should ply its trade enthusiastically with both hawk and gun. Unlike falconry, the shooting of birds allows the bird dog a payoff for a point when it is allowed to fetch the bird. Most of the bird dogs I've known seem to enjoy getting their mouths full of feathers from time to time. This especially seems to be the case early in the season when the dogs are overanxious and the warm dry weather here in the West makes picking up a good scent and solid point more difficult.

Anyone who trains a falcon should be able to train a dog, and many good texts are available. However, it is unwise to train an eyas falcon and a young bird dog at the same time, thinking that they will "grow up" together. Both are unknown quantities,

Peregrine tiercel rousing. *Rick Kline*

and predicting their respective actions is impossible. A young falcon needs steady points and a seasoned dog to provide quality slips. Conversely, a veteran game hawk will keep game lying still in front of a young pointer and will give the falconer some margin for the errors that often occur until the dog is up to par.

A comment sometimes heard from visiting European falconers is that U.S. falconers have well-trained falcons and poorly trained dogs. To some extent, we cause our own problems by attempting to do it all. Training dogs properly requires a considerable investment of time and energy that goes beyond our limit. Because falconers are preoccupied with the actions of their birds, they are unlikely to stop a flight in order to reprimand a dog for its errors. This pattern, if allowed to continue, permits the dog to forget its job and develop bad habits. I have two solutions to the problem. One is to have your dog worked into form by a professional trainer and "fine tuned" when needed. The other is to buy a trained dog. Considering the highly demanding nature of flying falcons over pointing dogs and the money spent on other aspects of the sport, it seems a worthwhile investment. In real terms, the quality of one's sport and performance of one's falcon, in the arena of upland game, hinges on the dog.

The ideal kennel for a falconer might include a brace of wide-ranging pointers and a close-working dog to work deep cover and flush. In years past, I used an English Pointer and a Brittany Spaniel for hawking upland game. This team simultaneously provided close and long-range coverage of the ground. The Brittany not only pointed, but also doubled as a duck flusher and retriever.

11 Small Game Hawking

Somehow, Jon Denton and I had a way of arranging our college class schedules to allow for afternoon hawking during fall and winter. While our falconry pursuits were not conducted on a grand scale, our enthusiasm for the chase was genuine.

Jon was not your ordinary guy. By the age of sixteen, he had been to the Far East, crash-landed a plane on an arctic gravel bar, hunted and fished for most of the game species in the Northwest, collected eyas gyrfalcons, and trained a variety of hawks and falcons. Academically, our interests included field studies of prairie falcon biology. In addition, we shared a very special love for an endearing tiercel prairie called "Punky."

Because there was no single, dependable quarry for tiercels in our area, we reasoned out a method for encountering opportunities on a variety of quarry for "Punky." Over the course of a season, we mapped auto routes that took us past isolated hedgerows, open fields, ponds, railroad tracks, creek bottoms, ditches, small orchards, and croplands. By introducing ourselves to local landowners, we got permission to fly hawks on most of the best ground.

Our sorties were focused on spotting certain birds along back roads. Only "marked" quarry, birds that we knew to be in good locations before the flight started, were flown.

Western Oregon was not expansive and through our mixture of open field and hedgerow hawking, the tiercel responded to the conditions that we provided. Unlike situations where a falcon is habituated to fly over a pointer or some body of water, Jon and I became the visual stimulus. The tiercel learned to key on our behavior and actions. Our job, working as a coordinated team, was to provide a well-timed flush. Some days we simply ran through a field, two abreast, to rout out a flock of doves at the proper time. At other times, we might find ourselves crashing through blackberry bushes or squeezing quail out of a ditch using a pincher movement. Our aim was always to organize an attack from two points, one that left the quarry no option but to fly into the open.

The thick cover and scarcity of quarry made this one of the most demanding types of falconry that I have seen or practiced. In this situation, the hawk was only as good as the beaters. Just as importantly, the beaters were only willing to work hard for a falcon that would not quit without exerting a gallant effort. When everyone did his part, it was exhilarating and beautiful to behold.

We started another tradition during those days. If we were close to the little town of Airlie at sunset, we made it a point to stop at the general store, the only store in town. This was a classic one-room building with oiled, planked flooring. The large wood stove was fondly anticipated for warming our bones and drying our rain gear. Perched in an old chair, cold soft drink in hand, we'd watch and listen as the veteran T.V. reporter, Walter Cronkite, related the news of the day. It gave us a chance to keep up with current events, hear all the local gossip, and take time to reflect.

Those were simple, carefree days. I haven't forgotten how exciting falconry was then. It felt good to be challenged, to work hard, and to be successful. But in the final analysis, it was the unique camaraderie of our team that formed a lasting impression and provided me a solid foundation for future falconry.

Hunting is the essence of falconry. It is the ultimate objective of the lengthy training process already described. After bringing a game hawk into hunting condition, the falconer can experience the excitement of the chase and the sense of accomplishment that comes from watching one's protege perform in the field. If one selects the falcon best matched to the most abundant and accessible quarry, this substantial investment in time and effort are rewarded.

North American falconers are fortunate to have many interesting choices of game. It is simply a fact of nature, however, that there are many more small birds available than large ones. A number of smaller species common throughout the midcontinent are legal quarry. These include doves, quail, and snipe. Tiercels, especially prairies, peregrines, Barbarys, shaheens, and lannerets, are especially well-suited for hunting small quarry. The tiercel's speed and maneuverability allow it to match actions of an elusive prey. Some large falcons, as well as various hybrids, are also capable of catching smaller birds.

Small game hawking can provide a great introduction to hunting with falcons. This form of falconry is adaptable to diverse surroundings. Such hawking provides fast action and produces more frequent slips than duck or upland game hawking. Flights at small game feature speed, adroitness, and precise footing rather than sheer physical power. The quality of the flights, the drama, and the satisfactions equal those in any other type of game hawking.

This type of hawking may be a practical alternative for individuals who want to be involved in falconry but lack access to the game and terrain suitable for flying large falcons. Such hawking offers much of the quality and style of classical game hawking, yet requires neither wide expanse of open ground nor the services of a highly-trained pointer. This is essentially "bare bones" falconry, with little of the pomp and circumstance associated with traditional game hawking. Most kills are totally consumed by the falcon so there is little left for the table. But this aspect is not likely to deter dedicated sportsmen. For them, seeing a dashing tiercel put through its paces is a sufficient reward.

I became a proponent of small game hawking in the early 1970s, when I acquired a succession of tiercel prairies and was obliged to find hunting opportunities for them. I found the sport to be much more than a scaled-down version of classical falconry. Not only is such hawking demanding, but it also provides the falconer with the best possible training in hawking strategy. It is surprising that relatively few falconers have seriously pursued this convenient sport.

Small game hawks can hunt a variety of quarry. This type of hawking may be easier to practice than other forms, in terms of land and game requirements. In other respects, the sport is more difficult because of the training and sophistication required of the falcon. To be effective against small, elusive prey, the game hawk must be able to adapt to many different situations and evasive tactics; it also must develop precise footing ability. Small game hawking in enclosed country does not always promise the spectacle of a high pitch and sweeping stoop, but will certainly showcase the agility, wits, and determination that distinguish superior falcons.

Most kills do not come easily. The tiercel's work is difficult, and too many flights at easy pigeons may spoil it for chasing other quarry. The falconer should not expect to achieve more than modest scores, but each successful flight is likely to represent a significant accomplishment. Some tiercels so enjoy flying that they will wait-on for upwards of an hour. Hawking with any falcon or tiercel that flies for the fun of it always makes for an exciting outing.

DOVES

Some small game birds live in wide-open country where they may be hawked in the same way as larger quarry. The most prominent member of this group is the mourning dove. Common throughout North America, the mourning dove occupies varied habitats and may sometimes be found on barren ground.

For defense against predators, doves have a loose, powdery plumage that is very slippery in a falcon's foot. Doves can vary their escape speeds, depending on how great a threat the falcon appears to be, and they have a particularly effective sideslip, often used when a falcon is only inches away from tagging them. Provided that the falcon is slipped at a distance of 100 to 200 yards, doves will hold tight until flushed. Few birds can match the impression of speed given by a flushing dove. The high speed escape is quite effective, but a slower, more hesitant, or indecisive departure may be an invitation for a hard strike. The dove's repertoire of evasive maneuvers makes it a challenging quarry for either tiercel or falcon, but one that can be matched by a decent game hawk. A direct hit on one of these birds invariably results in a shower of plumage.

The most fun I ever had hawking doves happened with my eyas tiercel prairie, Punky. I had located a weed-covered field that was used by all of the doves in the neighborhood. They were there every day, and it was an easy matter to mark a group coming in to feed. I would release the intermewed tiercel at the end of the field, then the dogs and I would flush the marked quarry or quarter the field in unison with the falcon waiting-on obediently overhead. The tiercel would not chase doves that flushed wild, preferring to maintain its position over the beaters until a dove flushed at my feet. Punky would instantly roll over and drive into the flushing dove, causing an explosion of feathers and leaving the disabled dove on the ground. If the dove wasn't killed outright, or was subsequently caught in cover, this tiercel would wait patiently for me to arrive before beginning the meal. On one outing, this remarkable game hawk caught a sparrow and disappeared for ten minutes. When he returned to the lure, he was still carrying the sparrow perfectly intact.

SNIPE

Another fine, open-country bird is the common snipe. These speedsters prefer moist ground with sparse, low vegetation. I have found snipe in the winter in plowed fields where they were congregating and feeding by the hundreds. They also frequent marshes, dairy pastures, flooded fields, ponds, and small creeks. Snipe tend to hold very tightly with a falcon in the air; it is sometimes necessary to nearly step on snipe to get them to flush. Some dogs will point them well, allowing the falconer to flush at the perfect time. More often, it may be necessary to run through fields and flush them at random with the aid of dogs. This is an unpredictable form of flying, but snipe are difficult to detect, even in plowed fields. When flocks of migrating snipe are frequenting an area, this type of hunting pays off. For some unknown reason, the places where I hawked snipe would "dry up" sporadically. Later, the same areas would suddenly be full of birds again. Perhaps this was the result of the snipe's daily activities or feeding habits.

For years I considered snipe to be impossible quarry. I now realize that my birds just had not seen enough snipe through the course of a season to learn how to hawk them successfully. No doubt my early impression was typical of falconers whose chance encounters with difficult quarry leave them with feelings of inadequacy.

I simply didn't know enough about the places where snipe congregate and the type of cover (the sparser, the better) where they should be hawked for optimum style and results. It is all too common to see a tiercel whizzing down after a snipe, only to have the snipe juke at the last second and head for the sky. But once a falcon begins pressing the snipe hard in the stoop, they begin to falter.

It is best to start a promising snipe hawk in areas with some ground cover. I've learned from experience that many snipe being chased by a competent game hawk will put in to cover. These are the snipe one should really press. They are the weak-hearted ones that are easiest to kill.

If the cover is too thick, it may be extremely difficult to get good reflushes. The snipe will put down every time the falcon attempts a strike. As long as the beaters persevere, however, the snipe should eventually fly. If the falconer gets the chance to grab the snipe by hand, the bird should be served immedimediately to the falcon. As with all other game hawking, once the falcon knows that the quarry is good to eat, it will press the chase even harder. As the novice falcon learns more about the quarry, the falconer can look forward to better flights under more demanding conditions.

QUAIL

North American quail represent a diverse group of upland game birds that are best classified as small game for falconry purposes. As a group, quail lack the speed and maneuverability to outfly a stooping falcon, and their frames cannot withstand the impact of a hard strike. Despite these characteristics, quail are sporting to hunt and are a suitable small game quarry. These birds inhabit brushy areas and, consequently, may only be caught at a disadvantage when they wander too far from cover. In places where vegetation is bunched, quail are vulnerable when they cross open ground.

Whether hunting Gambel and scaled quail in the desert Southwest or bobwhite in the Midwest, the quarry is a brush-hugger. Most of my experiences have been with California quail on the West Coast. These birds are often near water and take refuge in blackberry bushes growing in huge tangled masses, making the quail impervious to attack by a falcon. Most hunting opportunities will depend on the falconer's ability to locate a covey living along a fence line, hillside, railroad track, or mixed terrain of brush and cultivated ground. Ideally, quail are pointed by a dog in the open and are flown in the classic style. More often than not, the falconer will hear the quail or see them running near cover. They are seldom far from some form of sanctuary, but the sanctuary does not always prove to be secure. One or two good spaniels will roust them out of poor cover in short order, giving the falcon an eyeful of plump little bodies and whirring wings from which to choose. Tiercels love to chase quail, so even if the flight turns into a "rat hunt," the falcon will stay with the falconer in hopes of getting that one clean shot in the open. Often, the final stoop is a high speed sprint. Several times, I have seen tiercels grab a quail within inches of the brush and pull up just in time to avoid colliding with a thorny bush.

Quail may be found in open farm land, grasslands, and deserts across the continent. The greatest variety of quail, and perhaps the most suitable quail hawking terrain, is found in the Southwest. As a group, quail are prone to run to escape danger. They can be unpredictable for a pointer when in large groups, while holding much better as singles. Quail can also be difficult to keep in the air under a falcon, so that a pitch of 150 to 300 feet is adequate under most circumstances. Often the flights involve repeated stoops followed by numerous reflushes before a quail is taken. Bobwhites and Mearns quail are probably the best for hawking over pointers.

STARLINGS

I would be remiss if I did not mention pursuit of the ubiquitous starling. Like the English sparrow, the starling population now extends across the entire width and breadth of the U.S. and into parts of Canada and Mexico. The bird is a bona fide pest. Unfortunately, these birds have replaced native avifauna for important reasons: Starlings eat anything, they fill an unoccupied niche, they are tough, and they are smart!

I've never heard of a trained prairie falcon or peregrine that could consistently catch starlings. This is not to say that it can't be done, but it is a formidable undertaking. The task is difficult largely because starlings either flush as soon as the falcon is airborne, or they refuse to leave cover. Either response can be very frustrating for the hawking party. It is their intelligence that makes it difficult to engineer a kill from a pitch.

J. G. Mavrogordato discusses flights at starling in his classic work, *A Falcon in the Field*. He suggests the use of small, fast tiercels, like the Barbary or shaheen, which are capable of chasing starlings to cover straight from the fist. These tiercels then mount over the spot and stoop at the game when flushed. This sounds like classy falconry, and I fully intend to try it someday with the right falcon. I'm inclined to believe that the gyr/merlin or peregrine/merlin hybrid has incredible potential for this sport. However, tiercel prairie falcons don't seem to have the top-end speed needed to overhaul starlings in the open. Mavrogordato's suggestion for this dilemma when flying slower tiercels is to start the falcon out of sight and approximately half a mile away from the starlings. One encourages the tiercel to wait-on as high as possible, at least 400 feet, before bringing the falcon over the starlings and initiating the flush. Under some conditions, the starlings will linger long enough to allow the flight to work.

On precious few occasions have I pinned starlings in a bush or marked them down in stubble or sage. However, most of my flights at starlings were opportunistic encounters. Typically, my waiting-on falcon would spot a flock of starlings in an open, sometimes plowed, field and catch them unaware. I had one small prairie falcon that took starlings with relative ease from large flocks. While chasing ducks near dairies and feed lots, this falcon would inevitably stoop from a fine pitch and pluck a starling from one of the seething masses that were scavenging for food. I realize now that I should have plied her natural talents and pursued this quarry exclusively, but I was intent on applying her fine flight style to more traditional quarry. I must add a note of caution about this quarry. In certain locales, starlings are poisoned. In addition, some starling populations may maintain high levels of pesticides and mercury in their fat. These chemicals pose a risk to falcons that might feed on them. But generally, the sheer abundance and challenge of starlings make them a prospective quarry for the diligent falconer.

FERAL PIGEONS

Feral pigeons make good quarry and may be flown like game birds with highflying falcons. Next to the starling, the feral pigeon is the most abundant bird suitable for hawking. As with the starling, some slick maneuvering may be required to get the falcon into position above the pigeon before it flies.

In farm country, feral pigeons may be found feeding in grain fields, feedlots, pastures, and the like. Grain fields are probably the best setup, as pigeons appear to find comfort in the low, dense cover. These are perfect opportunities for flying marked quarry, and pigeons nearly always try to outfly the falcon instead of using cover.

Pigeons may also be found under bridges and in barns, hay sheds, or silos. If the falconer scouts the structure for birds from a distance, the pigeons will not become alarmed and leave. The falcon is loosed and allowed to mount in advance of the rush to flush the birds from their roosts.

Under some conditions, the falcon may try to engage in mind games with the pigeons. Some falcons play it straight, while others, particularly tiercel prairies, may enjoy chasing the pigeons high into the sky.

The mass of birds may mill around while the falcon is constantly mounting and appearing to take a nonchalant attitude toward the quarry. When one of the pigeons tries to drop back to earth, the falcon comes to life and the race is on. Similarly, some falcons mount in a particular area while the pigeons race around in circles. It sometimes appears that the pigeons are playing with the falcon, but if they get too testy and enter the "strike zone," they may forfeit their lives.

By intentionally hawking feral pigeons, the falconer may encourage an otherwise steady game hawk to rake away at inopportune moments. It is most annoying to mark down upland game in good cover or find a dog on point, and then see your falcon race off to a nearby barn to chase pigeons. In addition, feral pigeons, like starlings, pose health risks for the falcon.

Serious pigeon fanciers hold their birds in the same esteem that we hold ours. They can legally protect them from predators. A trained falcon is apt to meet a grim end if it encounters one of these people without the falconer nearby.

STRATEGY

Small game hawking is a sport requiring skill and discipline. The falconer must know how to interpret a variety of hunting situations, and be able to arrange each flight to take advantage of the terrain, cover, and the characteristics of the quarry. After suitable game has been located, it is often necessary to flush the game repeatedly from cover with which it is intimately familiar. The game hawk must know its part well and must assist the falconer, keeping pressure on the quarry and pinning it down until a good flush can be made. Often quarry will put in to escape being killed; reflushes then depend on the size of the quarry and the amount of cover. The falcon must wait-on obediently for a clean attack opportunity. Extensive cover or unflushable quarry can end the flight and demoralize the falcon. As a result, the falcon may drop its pitch considerably or quit chasing altogether.

Most of the quarry encountered in small game hawking will stay close to cover because it can't outfly the falcon in level flight. The quarry is painfully aware of this fact and tries to avoid being flushed into the open. Many game birds drive themselves into the scantiest cover in search of refuge. Others will fly along the contours of the brush as the falcon begins to stoop so that they can disappear a split second before the strike. Often the contest is one of stamina as the hawking team tries to wear down the quarry; with repeated reflushes the quarry will tire. The presence of the falcon is enough to intimidate most small game birds into holding like a rock. When the noise and confusion become too great, they panic into flight. At other times, they start to flush, then change their minds and try to regain cover. Either situation can give the falcon the upper hand momentarily and allow it to put a foot on the quarry. "He who hesitates" with a falcon overhead is generally lost. Nevertheless, some small game species adeptly maintain control and win their escape, despite all the chaos.

Small game birds can take advantage of many different types of cover. Some will pin down in the open fields, while others use stubble, hedgerows, or tall grass as camouflage. Small trees and bushes are common hangouts for small birds, and they may seek such refuges when hard pressed by the falcon. Reflushes from isolated cover, when coupled with a handful of rocks, are often effective. In practice, chasing birds from a lone tree or bush in the open is in many ways similar to hawking ducks from a pond. The birds are forced into a compromising position and, having made good their immediate escape by avoiding a stoop, choose to return to their sanctuary because of intimidation. One may then repeat the process for additional flights.

Generally, singles hold better than flocks, a tendency that works to the falconer's advantage. For young falcons, more time should be devoted to finding one or two birds, preferably young ones. Unfortunately, it seems that all too often an inexperienced falcon starts at one bird and ends up chasing new ones with each ensuing flush. For a novice game hawk, it is a good practice to isolate one prospective bird and concentrate on flushing it perfectly. Should the falconer succeed in locating a small group of birds, there may be a decent chance of picking one out, and pushing it to the bitter end. In cover, a large group of birds may prefer to stay together for safety and sit just as tightly as a single. Like shooting at a flock of ducks, the hunter must take aim at only one bird at a time if any are to drop.

LOCATING SMALL GAME

Particularly for the suburban falconer with a small game hawk, there are three prerequisites for pursuing the sport: getting permission to use land, planning daily hawking routes, and locating pockets of game that consistently produce flights. When approached by a sincere falconer asking for the privilege of land access, most property owners agree. It is then necessary to reinforce this trust with gestures of good will, such as leaving fences intact and closing gates. A holiday card, some fresh game, or a supply of their favorite beverage may be helpful in this regard. Many suburban falconers keep a low profile when hawking in order to avoid undue attention and unwelcome interference.

It is important for the falconer to maximize his or her time in the field. Depending on road access and distance to good

Eyas peregrine tiercel with snipe. *Rick Kline*

hawking country, the falconer should try to establish several routes through areas with high probabilities of slips. One or two of these routes can be covered daily, and it should not take long to find the most productive areas. Sometimes these areas provide only one or two flights, but occasionally this system produces a hot spot. Quarry can be expected to move seasonally in response to changes in weather, cover height, and food availability.

In this type of hawking, pockets of game may be found in an overgrown pasture, a weed patch, or several hundred square feet of stubble. These places naturally attract small birds and are helpful for keeping a good falcon steady by virtue of the consistent rewards provided. It is best not to overwork such places, as game tends to thin out if the birds are hawked every day. Allow prime areas a day or two of rest between flights. This practice also permits the game to become more at ease and less likely to flush prematurely when the silhouette of a falcon appears in the sky.

Falconers who live in marginal country for flying falcons might consider enhancing habitat by clearing out open patches in thick cover, establishing water sources, or by planting cover and food crops for their preferred quarry. Common wildlife management techniques can often be used effectively. Through such efforts, populations of game may be attracted and artificially supported in locations that are favorable for flights.

Good hawking country should provide an unobstructed view of the falcon and allow the chase to continue safely. To lose sight of the falcon not only spoils the fun, but may also lead to the loss of a trained bird. Man-made obstacles such as telephone wires, power lines, and fences of all kinds have proved lethal to many game hawks. These obstacles should be steadfastly avoided. One need not live on the moors of Scotland to practice falconry, but considerable discretion and common sense must be exercised by the suburban falconer to protect a game hawk in the field.

12 Duck Hawking

There are days when things just go right. For me, these days come later in the season when the falcon is in really top form. By then the hawking team is coordinated, giving the falcon greatest advantage at every flight.

All season long, Brad Mitchell and I had been hawking ducks seriously. It had been a painfully slow season and we had invested long hours and many miles behind the wheel in search of precious few duck slips. Because game was scarce, we had tempered our hunting lust by feeding the falcon generously from each kill. This kept her motivated during the lean times. The migration was late and our hawking season was rapidly drawing to a close. Toward the end of December, storms on the Pacific coast forced a whole new population of ducks inland to our fresh water ponds. Suddenly, wintering ducks were in full force and we were privy to an unusual but short-lived abundance of quarry.

By early winter, Kudu, my intermewed passage prairie falcon, had been on the wing for several months and was exceptionally fit. A veteran of many duck-hawking seasons, her forte seemed to be keeping pressure on the ducks wherever they might be. It's been my experience that intermewed falcons, like fine wine, improve with age. At this point, the falcon was at her prime.

There is something delightful about peering over the edge of a series of ponds and seeing the surface fully covered with ducks. That is how it was this day. I released the falcon from the car and casually filled one pocket with rocks as she began mounting over the water. The plan called for us to circle to the south and force the ducks out over the pasture instead of toward the paved road. But while crossing the fence, we scared a handful of ducks from a side pond; they paddled and launched into the air. Kudu stooped instantly and struck a scaup down below the bank. I crawled below the elevated dike and picked up the falcon with a quail. With the season drawing to a close, and because there were more ducks than we had seen in one place all year, we decided to press on. I put Kudu up a second time. Again, ducks from one of the side ponds flushed and Kudu's stoop saw another scaup struck down and captured.

A unique situation was developing for us. We now had two ducks in the bag and hundreds more just out of sight over the lip of the large, elevated pond. The falcon had flown twice in less than ten minutes, killed two ducks in efficient stoops, and wasn't even getting a workout. What to do? We held a short meeting and promptly threw our conservative notions about falconry to the wind. Up went the falcon. I vaguely remember having to wave my arms in a threatening manner to encourage the next group of ducks to flush. As is typical of frightened ducks, they went every direction. We intentionally flushed with the falcon wide and, typically, Kudu stooped as soon as the ducks started to fly. I saw her cutting a sharp angle, pumping her wings hard all the way down, and lining up a target. Suddenly, there was a tremendous crash as the chosen bird was struck and literally bounced off the metal roof of a pump house. The duck dribbled to the ground where it was promptly collected by Kudu. Three up, three down. I hurried over to retrieve the victor and vanquished, yet another scaup.

I suddenly came to the realization that I wasn't teaching this intermewed falcon anything new. In fact, it was I who was learning about the effects of time and experience on a game hawk's psyche.

For the fourth time, I loosed the falcon and she took yet another commanding pitch over the complex of ponds. Once again, ducks flushed perfectly and the falcon, in an economy of motion and practiced efficiency, struck down her fourth duck in a single stoop. The game bag was now heavily laden and we had been in the field a total of twenty-five minutes.

While many people feel it is unfair to compare a fine falcon to anything mechanical or man-made, this performance showed elements of pure precision. As with any art form, mastery leaves onlookers with the impression that the performance was easy. In this case, it had only taken me twenty years of study, and Kudu six years of training, to orchestrate such a fluid performance.

Duck hawking at ponds offers excellent sport under controlled conditions. The objective is to locate ducks on small bodies of water, release the falcon and have it wait-on high above the water, then flush the ducks for the falcon to chase. Ducks are fast and maneuverable in the air. Because they fly to escape danger and bypass ground cover when under attack, the falcon's stoop often terminates in a dramatic, high speed collision of predator and prey. Ducks spotted on the water are essentially marked game, but unlike upland game birds, pursued ducks will consistently return to the same body of water from which they were flushed. As a result, it is frequently possible to repeatedly flush the same birds under the same set of conditions. Given good setups over small ponds, the average falcon will catch ducks regularly. On the other hand, even the most experienced game hawk may be challenged when flown on ducks over large bodies of water. By varying the hunting conditions, the falconer can test the falcon's endurance and determination.

Small, shallow ponds in flat terrain devoid of trees and ground cover present some of the most ideal conditions for hunting ducks. I love to turn a veteran "duck hawk" loose at a small pond that it knows well.

An experienced falcon invariably heads straight for the water and mounts above the pond. Always keeping the ducks in view, it circles higher and wider while the falconer gets into position for the flush. When the quarry springs from the water, the falcon pumps all the way down and delivers a solid, debilitating blow to the duck. Such a falcon can make the sport look deceptively easy. Unfortunately, these ideal conditions are few and far between, and wedding a falcon to ducks is often a complicated matter.

Because ducks characteristically return to water when pursued, duck hawking can be very frustrating for the falcon. After repeatedly failing to kill, any game hawk will become discouraged. Young and inexperienced falcons soon show signs of extreme demoralization. Splashes from escaping ducks that dive headlong into the water can make the falcon water-shy and further degrade performance. A falcon will remain enthusiastic if it is confident that the falconer will continue to produce good hunting opportunities. If repeatedly denied the satisfaction of a kill, the falcon will lose heart and fail to press the attack.

The obvious approach for building the falcon's confidence is to set up the early flights on the smallest ponds available. The setup should allow the falcon to strike the quarry well away from the water. The duck may be stunned but not killed on the first stoop. Once knocked down, a duck is disoriented and usually caught by the falcon on the second pass.

The falcon should be waiting-on directly over the water when the ducks are flushed. Attempt to make a "blind side" approach whenever possible in order to get close to the ducks without flushing them prematurely. If the pond is diked or sunken, it may be possible to move in undetected. A carefully timed flush, with sudden noise to confuse and frighten the ducks off the water at the right moment, should have them leaving the pond according to plan.

After the flush, it is important for the falconer to be positioned between the duck and the small pond to assist the falcon as necessary. If the duck avoids the stoop and returns to the pond, it may be possible to make it flare or to quickly wade in and reflush. It may also be necessary for the falconer to help the falcon dispatch the duck quickly, especially if the duck is large. If the falcon gets "wing whipped" by the quarry, it possibly could refuse to chase ducks again. On occasion, the falconer may grab a duck that was hit by the falcon or hidden in the brush. Whenever that occurs, the duck should be impeded and served to the falcon over open ground. It is crucial that a new falcon be convinced that ducks are good to eat and can be caught with reasonable effort. One should not be concerned with pitch or style now, so long as the falcon stays interested.

Medium-sized puddle ducks and divers are the easiest quarry for the inexperienced falcon to kill. As a group, they tend to hold well with the falcon overhead, and they have a predictable flying style. Furthermore, they are not as likely as small ducks, such as teal, to drop into cover and spoil the falcon's stoop. Once the game hawk begins to kill regularly, it may then be presented more difficult flights over larger ponds. After the falcon has killed a dozen or so ducks, the falconer will have a good indication of its talent, tenacity, and dedication.

To keep the falcon's spirits up, the falconer should allow generous feedings from the early kills, especially during its first season. Later, it may be primed sporadically with gorges on duck. When my own game hawks have failed to kill after great effort at big water hawking for two or three days in a row, I take them to a small pond, allow an easy kill and gorge them. This procedure works wonders for their attitude and has been known to improve the manners and style of even veteran duck hawks.

STRATEGY

Whether a pond is twenty feet or 200-feet wide, the principles of flushing ducks remain the same. Fortunately for the falconer, most bodies of water are irregular in shape. The primary objective is to push the ducks over dry land on the first flush. If that fails, the ducks must be herded into the smallest section of water and eventually pushed out over land on successive reflushes. This often requires a series of testing flights. Ducks are usually intimidated by the presence of a falcon and will try to remain on the water for self-defense. If the falcon stays too close, the ducks will fly only as a last resort. If the falcon is too far away, the ducks may escape altogether. By trial and error, the falcon must learn to find its own best initial distance from the quarry. Meanwhile, the falconer must try to get the ducks to take to the air by shouting and clapping hands, throwing rocks, and using any other scare tactics available.

This is always a fun part of duck hawking. Each falcon develops its own unique way of dealing with the situations presented. A falcon that will "sky out" upwind may give the ducks the impression that it is no longer interested in them. As soon as the ducks have flown clear of the water, such a falcon will stoop across the sky to overhaul them. This tactic obviously calls for a great deal of learning by the falcon. If it stoops too soon, the ducks will return to the water and spoil the attack.

Good falcons often take matters into their own hands, herding ducks around the sky. By "feinting" with false stoops over distances of 100 to 200 feet, these falcons panic the ducks into evasive action and often split the flock into sections. When one of the groups eventually flies too far over land, the falcon drops out of the sky and pounds a duck into the ground. I have also had falcons that would take a pitch of 200 to 400 feet and wait-on, appearing to ignore the ducks completely until they had just cleared the bank of the pond. Then the falcon would instantly "turn on" and cut one down. On the other hand, some falcons, such as my old game hawk Kudu, use "sheep dog" tactics to maintain constant pressure on ducks. These harassment techniques are not as aesthetically pleasing to watch, but do ensure that the falcon is close to the ducks when they finally decide to leave the safety of the pond. Such hawking can also be exhausting for both the falconer and the game hawk because the ducks may drop back on the water repeatedly and must be reflushed time and again. Incidentally, such tactics are often helpful when hawking large flooded fields. The presence of the falcon usually keeps the ducks pinned down while the falconer works toward them in the open.

In some areas, ducks may be hawked while feeding in open fields. Slips on small groups in cut grain fields or other light cover are preferred. This type of hawking is similar to flights on upland game birds that have been marked down. The falcon should be released out of sight of the ducks, and the falconer should wait until it gains a good pitch before approaching the pinned quarry. One should run toward the ducks while the falcon is waiting-on either over the ducks or between them and the falconer. If the ducks should flush prematurely, the falcon still will have a reasonable chance of overhauling them.

Huge flocks of migrating ducks often congregate in cut grain fields. If stressed by cold weather, they seem oblivious to wild predators and adopt a safety-in-numbers strategy. A milling flock of 5,000 ducks can be very confusing to a falcon. However, a large number of visible prey circling a particular field presents another problem; the falcon may see no need to take a pitch when it is just as easy to fly into a low flock and bind to a duck. Here proper presentation becomes the objective.

To encourage a falcon to take a suitable pitch, there are two options. The first is to occupy the designated field well ahead of the typical feeding time, say late afternoon, and release the falcon before the ducks arrive. A falcon that waits-on for 30 to 40 minutes will already be in good position when the first ducks come in to eat. The second technique is to release the falcon a mile or more away from the field and lead it into position once the ducks arrive. Some falcons learn to follow the falconer's car and may be guided into position from several miles away.

It is also possible to hawk ducks in standing corn or in marshes, but this is strictly a labor of love. The falconer must run helter-skelter through heavy vegetation, attempting to flush game for the faithful falcon. After all this effort, much of the flight may be hidden from view, and the final results are often obscured by high cover.

In some parts of the U.S., the morning and evening feeding flights of waterfowl may provide the only opportunities to catch ducks. In the West, intense shooting pressure has conditioned waterfowl to lounge or raft in the middle of large rivers or reservoirs during the day. Similar situations may be encountered along the eastern shore of Chesapeake Bay and other eastern flyways. In such areas, the ducks find safe havens well out of gun range and remain inaccessible until they leave to feed.

In old English terms, "hawking at the brook" meant flying falcons at ducks chased off brooks or creeks. The sport was once popular in Britain, but few falconers in the U.K. have practiced it in recent years. I find it surprising that British falconers don't consider ducks as suitable game for falcons. My guess is that they simply haven't flown falcons at ducks, and don't realize how much fun it is.

Ditches, canals, and small meandering rivers can provide excellent slips at ducks. As with big water hawking, the sport tends to be physically demanding, because ducks can go for long distances along the water course before encountering a sharp turn, dike, culvert, or other impediment that forces them over dry land. To work these waters effectively, at least two people are required, and a good water dog is invaluable. The ducks must be pinched between the flushers, as in hawking upland or small game. Mallards and the larger divers tend to flush well from creeks, making a clean, one-stoop kill possible. On the other hand, teal flights will run everybody ragged. Small divers, like buffleheads and ruddy ducks, may start diving and refuse to fly altogether. It is always a judgment call to determine when to quit and look for a better setup. One can disappoint a falcon for only so long.

LOCATING DUCKS

Farm ponds, lakes, lagoons, old quarries, flooded fields, and irrigation canals are likely spots for finding ducks. Most dairy farms have a pond of some sort. Water can be found wherever there is livestock, especially in the arid West. In the high desert, ponds are often scooped out in otherwise flat terrain to trap

Haggard peregrine falcon. *Rick Kline*

runoff water. In addition, dry creek beds are dammed and slightly dished to serve as watering tanks for range cattle. In northern latitudes, many of these waters will freeze in early winter and become unsuitable for waterfowl. One must then look for ducks on the spring-fed or swiftly running creeks and waterways that remain open in sub-zero temperatures. In winter, geothermal ponds and creeks are likely to attract large flocks, and are excellent sites for cold weather duck hawking.

When searching for places to fly falcons on ducks, I usually look first for "NO HUNTING!" signs. In recent years, such signs have been appearing with increasing frequency at farms, ranches, and other privately owned ground. In most cases, these lands have been posted to prohibit public shooting. If approached politely, the owners will often allow a falconer to fly game hawks although some may prefer that the dog be left behind to avoid frightening the livestock. Most often, this privilege means access to ducks and other game birds that flock to such refuges.

Without question, the most rapid and efficient way to locate suitable ponds for duck hawking is to survey from the air. By flying, the falconer will acquire a special feel for the lay of the land and discover ponds that may have been unknown for years. With a good map and a knowledge of the landmarks, it is simple to plot the locations of ponds and mark the best routes for access. Some years ago, Chris Merker and I scouted our hawking area with a light plane. In a ten-minute flight, we were able to assess an area that would otherwise require hours by car. Admittedly, airplanes are quite expensive, but there is no better way to explore those out-of-the-way ponds.

13 Upland Game Hawking

Much of what is written about falconry is accepted as gospel by its followers. This body of knowledge fortifies the established doctrines and, for the most part, is responsible for directing falconers to a means of success. There are, however, other dimensions to the sport that, for whatever reasons, continue to be overlooked or unimagined. All forms of game hawking, for example, involve a common theme: the falcon takes a pitch overhead, then game is driven out and attacked in a high-speed stoop. Yet, there are endless variations on this theme. I encourage falconers to break new ground, seek individual philosophies, and look for unique combinations of falcons, quarry, dogs, and land to broaden the scope of falconry.

The challenge of hawking upland game in the high desert foothills of southern Idaho caused me to rethink my approach to falconry. Honest game birds, open country, and good weather formed the foundation for this undertaking. Locally, our weather early in the season is hot and dry. While fine for duck hawking, these conditions present extremely difficult conditions for pointing dogs. The dogs do not run well in the heat and bird scent is difficult to locate. So, for me, the choice of quarry is seasonal and the pursuit of upland game, particularly Hungarian partridge, has become a cold weather sport.

I learned a new approach to upland game hawking with Jasmine, a passage red-naped shaheen that I flew for seven seasons. Salvaged from a hawk market in the Middle East and given to me by my friend Charles H. Schwartz, she was a stroke of good fortune. As falcons go, Jasmine was small and compact, with a flying weight around 24 1/2 ounces. She waited-on high and steady, was fast and flew with cunning; truly, a falcon for all seasons.

Jasmine seemed equally fond of waterfowl and upland game, adding greatly to the variety of our hawking. By late November, most of the ponds were frozen and the ground moisture needed for good dog work was provided by rain and snow. Up to this point, the falcon enjoyed the luxury of unhurried, marked flights at ducks. She was strong on the wing, accustomed to taking her time gaining a pitch before game was served, and confident in my ability to flush quarry that could be killed.

At her peak of condition and confidence, she had what I call the "gorilla" mentality. In this mindset, Jasmine flew with enthusiasm and purpose, waited-on dutifully for an hour or more, and chased any quarry that she saw. There were, however, two drawbacks to this situation. First, she might refuse to come down and end the flight until she had killed. The second drawback, infinitely more troublesome, was that if she was served a pigeon that did not outclimb her and leave the vicinity, she would chase it out of sight. Once she flew one of my homing pigeons for over ten miles. On such occasions, if she caught the pigeon or didn't come back, I was forced to track her down, which put the falcon at risk until I arrived to collect her. I adopted methods to avoid these problems. To temper her intensity and aggression, I increased Jasmine's flying weight by about half an ounce and flew earlier in the day. I also released only well-conditioned, experienced pigeons and never served a free-flighted pigeon within an hour of darkness. Many falcons go into panic hunting as dusk approaches and will persistently chase any quarry that stays in the air.

Balancing falconry with a family, a career, and all of the other aspects of life is not easy. I suspect this balancing act will be the greatest challenge for working falconers in the future. For me, December to February is the most trying time to hawk. After daylight saving time ends, there is less time to hawk, without scheduling time away from work, and the falcon has fewer ideal opportunities at quarry. It is imperative to get a good start early in the season in order to carry the falcon through the more difficult periods later. With Jasmine, having less time in the field meant that our excursions had to be orderly experiences, translating into quality hawking time for the entire team.

During winter, partridge are the best available quarry in southwest Idaho. Fortunately, the Hungarian partridge is not a popular game bird for shooters; most are taken as incidentals to pheasant hunting. After November, one rarely encounters other people in good partridge habitat. My favorite hawking areas are ridges of cheatgrass and scattered stands of sagebrush. The slopes are rolling, often steep and cut by deep gullies. This seemingly desolate landscape with few roads, sparse cover, and little snowfall is home to partridge, but they are rarely seen. I began pressing an older English Pointer and Brittany Spaniel into service, neither of which had much prior experience with partridge. They tried hard and found birds, but often false pointed.

The standard approach to hawking upland game is to have a dog establish a point before the falcon is released. It takes a good pointer to locate partridge, and a staunch, careful dog not to flush the birds prematurely. Often, partridge are found in areas of no visible cover. They survive in these places only because of their furtive behavior and camouflaged plumage. Eventually, I discovered that a nontraditional approach to upland game hawking worked better for me. My dogs were not always reliable, and I soon learned that the longer Jasmine flew, the higher she went. It became clear that if I wanted to see exceptional stoops from lofty pitches, I needed to be patient about flushing the game.

My eventual routine was to begin from the top of the ridge on the downwind side of the hawking ground. With the perfunctory tasks completed, I loosed the falcon and released the dogs. A game of "find the pointer" then commenced. These hikes would often cover four or five miles and last several hours. It was imperative that I carried a variety of falconry gear with me, so I began adapting my gear for these forced marches. First, I modified the telemetry gear with a scabbard for the antenna and a waist pack for the receiver. Next, I replaced my traditional hawking bag with a lightweight hawking vest, complete with large gusseted pockets made of webbing and small equipment pouches. The vest made it possible to carry four large pigeons and all my other paraphernalia in relative comfort, and did not bang against my legs as I ran or climbed hills. By redistributing the load, I was able to eliminate the sore neck muscles that had been caused by the shoulder strap of my hawking bag.

Some falconers may call this "flying on speculation." But I don't consider it so because I know that as many as ten coveys of partridge live within a 5-square mile area. One of the early references to this practice is found in *Falconry* by Gilbert Blaine. Because Scottish red grouse would not hold for a point late in the season, he flew a reliable falcon over the moor to scare the grouse and make them hold for the dog.

My activities were an adaptation of his theory to my conditions. My dogs would sometimes locate a skittish pheasant that wandered into the desert. Caught in the open and unable to run due to lack of cover, these pheasants were at a disadvantage. With a snappy point and a well-timed flush, it was an enjoyable way to hawk such slippery quarry.

Another factor in practicing this form of falconry was that I began to crave the exercise. More and more, I detested hawking by driving around for miles. To waste gasoline and pollute the air under the guise of outdoor recreation is, to me, a moral conflict. There is no more enjoyable physical therapy for a middle-aged falconer with a desk job and a bad back than hiking behind a big running pointer. Driving up to a dog on point, rushing a falcon into position, and sprinting in for a fast flush all lack any semblance of aesthetic appeal for me. Instead, I relished those walks through the hills, interacting with the falcon and dogs, drinking in the vista, reading the sky, and being alone but not lonely.

The development and perpetuation of this hunting style hinged on the facts that Jasmine was a perfect match for partridge and she loved to fly. In thirty years of falconry, I have never seen a falcon that so delighted in the exhilaration of flying high and stooping fast. I quickly learned that my job was to maintain her interest. Cultivating patience and an extremely high pitch in a game hawk takes several seasons, and is not without its risks. Jasmine was a quick study, but she was also fond of attacking passing pigeons or ducks. For that reason, I had to be cautious about where I flew her. A compounding problem was that I used racing pigeons as substitute quarry during the winter. While I could not rely on my dogs to immediately locate birds to fly, I could keep the falcon's attention with pigeons while we searched the hills for a point. I kept track of the time the falcon was in the air, and I would toss a pigeon about every twenty minutes if we hadn't found game for her to chase. Pigeons took her up into the sky and outflew her. This escape tactic, the opposite of what upland game birds use against avian predators, is what seemed to keep Jasmine flying in the proper style between points. If pressed for an explanation, I would say that the falcon needed to chase quarry that could outfly her in order for her to remain aware of the value of pitch.

What is the proper style for partridge hawking? That depends on terrain and cover. In our open desert, there is no such thing as a pitch that is too high. A falcon that waits-on at a mere 200 or 300 feet will either cause partridge to crash repeatedly into cover or be promptly outflown by the quarry. Jasmine showed me that a falcon waiting-on high overhead has distinct advantages. In some cases, I don't think the partridge knew she was coming. Even when they did, they were unable to judge the speed of her attack.

One of Jasmine's more effective maneuvers was to stoop down close to the ground, then slingshot up into the covey. This effectively cut the birds off from cover while they were going too fast to land. Did Jasmine know that this attack style would prevent the partridge from escaping? Clearly, she did. In these instances, she invariably bound to the partridge with a hard, audible chink of her bells. With the momentum of these stoops, she occasionally pitched up high into the air carrying her prey or cut a large circle, bleeding off speed as she prepared to land and dispatch her quarry on the ground. Jasmine's feet were large in proportion to her body. Once she had a partridge in her grasp, it never came loose. The high pitch also made it possible for her to overhaul wild-flushed quarry. Eventually, it became more interesting to flush when the falcon was wide of the pointer and watch her streak across the sky to overtake game. If the quarry escaped, she simply went back up for another try.

Over time, Jasmine became a pillar of dependability. I recall that on one afternoon she flew for two hours, stooping at partridge and remounting repeatedly out of binocular range after putting them into cover. Her stoops often went from horizon to horizon, and were dazzling and noisy affairs, sounding like she was ripping the sky open with her wings. It is difficult to estimate just how high Jasmine was flying on her best days. Based on the fact that her quarry was sometimes 500 yards away before she got down to it, I would guess that she was between 3,000- and 4,000-feet high on such days. The most memorable time that I saw this pitch put to good use was while exploring rugged, new ground with Eric Tabb. Jasmine was feeling her oats and had wandered off, mounting higher and higher into a beautiful blue, late-winter sky. The telemetry told us that she was not leaving, so we let her fly as we traversed the crest of the long, steep ridge. Suddenly, the dog bumped a single partridge, just below us but near the top of the ridge. The terrain looked like a giant ski jump falling away below us and the partridge headed straight down slope at full throttle. About eight seconds later, we heard the falcon coming in from above and behind the ridge. She leveled off over our heads momentarily at about 800 feet, then stooped straight down in front of us. By now, the partridge was well down the hill and going all-out. We watched as Jasmine closed the gap, a tight little teardrop traveling at terminal velocity. It was such an odd perspective, watching a falcon stooping at prey from above. Hundreds of yards away, at the very bottom of the ridge, the partridge banked to turn out of the draw. Just as it flattened out and veered to the right, probably thinking it was home free, Jasmine bound to it. It was not until we reached the bottom and found Jasmine with her prize that we realized she had taken her first wild chukar partridge. Such days convinced me that falconry is the ultimate spectator sport.

Ralph Waldo Emerson wrote that "consistency is the hobgoblin of little minds." From a falconer's perspective, I cannot agree. Consistency in a trained falcon means reliability in the field. Game hawking, as an art form, seeks to bring order to the chaos of environmental variables and animal behavior. While there is little one can do about the weather, the actions of a falcon and dog can be influenced to repeat themselves in a desired sequence of events for one's benefit as a falconer.

The highlight of my falconry career was that I could teach and be taught by such a remarkable falcon as Jasmine. Our relationship, based on mutual confidence, was the ultimate compliment for any falconer. As a lad, I read many inspiring passages from my books about highflying falcons, quarry exploding from cover, and sizzling stoops from the heavens. This is the stuff of which a falconer's dreams are made, but with Jasmine, the dreams became a reality. I encourage you to experience this caliber of falconry for yourself. I have seen greatness in a trained falcon and it is a wonder.

The pursuit of upland game birds with a falcon and pointing dog is classical falconry in its truest sense. Game hawking allows the falconer to field a coordinated team and test it with challenging quarry. Nearly everyone involved in hunting upland game with longwings agrees that this teamwork is the most difficult yet most rewarding goal to which a falconer can aspire.

In principle, the methods of upland game hawking are similar to those outlined in the chapter on small game. However, there are some important differences. The larger game birds require larger falcons, and the need to fly medium-sized and large falcons imposes special demands for open hunting areas. As a result, careful planning becomes essential in order to cover larger areas efficiently and establish favorable hunting situations. In addition, the need for well-trained pointing dogs introduces an extra variable and complicates the falconer's task of controlling and coordinating the field. Compared to other forms of falconry, this type tends to be more formal and systematic, chiefly because it is often less forgiving of errors, oversights, and shortcuts. On balance, hawking upland game is a stylish and sophisticated sport, with pointing dogs adding an extra dimension of beauty, excitement, and fun.

The terrain best suited for this pursuit is open land with low vegetation. The hawking area should be devoid of people and far enough away from the structures of civilization to avoid any interference, distractions, and hazards to the game hawk. Ideally, the conditions will allow the falconer to search the area visually and listen for telltale sounds while trailing behind the pointer at a comfortable but steady pace. As one takes in the sights, sounds, and smells of the landscape, it is possible to tune out that other world, and enjoy the invigorating life of a falconer while getting into action with the team.

A talented bird dog will generate excitement by itself. The flashy ones range in full view as they cast back and forth, crisscrossing the ground in front of the falconer. They enjoy their work as much as any creature I know. The sudden stop or cautious creep to a stop is a welcome sight, for it is then that the falcon may be released with some assurance that an opportunity at game is forthcoming.

One of the side benefits to this type of hawking is the absence of distracting elements to sabotage the slip. A good dog will not point small birds. Most passerines lie low and stay out of sight once the falcon is airborne. So, barring a false point or the intrusion of an aggressive wild falcon, it is reasonable to expect a straightforward flush and stoop.

In addition to locating game, the dog's task is to give the falconer time to prepare for the flush. Naturally, the dog must not move until the falconer makes in or gives the dog permission to break point. Occasionally, a pointer may hold a point for more than twenty minutes, but one can't expect the quarry or the dog to remain all day in this position.

The old British falconry manuals stressed the importance of circling upwind of the dog in order to "head" the quarry. The falconer was supposed to walk into the point from upwind and flush the game birds downwind. I believe it is the position of the falcon, not the position of the beaters, that determines the escape route of the game. Provided that the falcon is at a decent pitch and dead overhead or slightly upwind, it will have ample opportunity to connect with the quarry. Heading is even less advantageous during windy conditions because the falconer has no idea how far the game lies ahead of the dog. One may miss the game by coming in too soon or, worse yet, cause them to flush at the wrong moment. Hordes of spectators can act as a wall to force the game in the desired direction. In many cases, however, game birds seem to flush in whatever direction they choose.

The falconer who hawks alone, as I generally do, is apt to have little influence on the birds' choice of direction. However, the falcon's position may influence the quarry's escape route. If the falcon has a good pitch and is slightly upwind, it will intercept the quarry before it has gone far. The falcon maintains its strategic advantage until the game bird builds up enough speed to negate the downward power of the stoop. Given enough room, the falcon may overhaul quarry such as pheasant or partridge that are flushed upwind. While there may be insufficient momentum left for the falcon to strike a killing blow, it may be possible for the falcon to bind to it. Prairie grouse use this opportunity to apply a burst of speed and head skyward.

Only a gyrfalcon or gyr hybrid is likely to keep up with them at such times.

Falconers have reached no consensus on whether it is more efficient for a game hawk to bind to or to strike quarry in the stoop. Many upland game birds seem capable of recovering quickly from less-than-lethal strikes. In areas with abundant cover, a falcon which binds to game may have less chance of losing it while going to ground. This is especially true of prairie grouse, for this quarry often can absorb blows that would devastate any other game bird, and then manage to outdistance its pursuer.

I prefer to see a falcon power down from a high pitch and drive right through its quarry. This karate-chop style of footing can be so forceful that the quarry doesn't even twitch when it hits the ground. Some falcons generate tremendous force from even a modest pitch, and exceptional falcons learn to kill by striking the head. While a hardhitting falcon runs the risk of injuring itself, the bird spends less time struggling with game, especially when it is outweighed by quarry such as cock pheasant or sage grouse.

GROUSE

Despite honest differences of opinions on some issues, almost all longwingers agree on the key attributes of the ideal quarry: The perfect game bird should live with a covey in open country where vegetation is sparse. The bird should hold well for a pointing dog, and it should always flush according to plan as a single, rather than in unison with other members of the covey. When flushed, the bird should strive to outmaneuver a falcon fairly in the air, using its powers of flight to outdistance the falcon. Each of these attributes works to the falconer's advantage. The group of gallinaceous game birds known as North America's prairie grouse comes closest to having all these features.

Unlike the legendary red grouse of Scotland, which is actually a ptarmigan rather than a grouse, the North American representatives of the grouse family are large, robust game birds with powers of flight unlike other quarry. Both the greater and lesser prairie chickens are residents of the Great Plains. Today, prairie chickens are found in restricted zones and cling tenaciously to those few prairie lands left intact.

The sharp-tailed grouse occupies diverse habitats ranging from tall grass and sagebrush prairies to the Boreal forest of Canada. Unlike true prairie grouse, sharp-tails need trees and brush as part of their wintering areas; buds, fruits, and catkins comprise much of their winter diet. In certain locales sharp-tailed grouse mix with prairie chickens, interbreeding where their ranges overlap. But farther north and west of the Rocky Mountains, the sharp-tail is the only bird of its type.

Sage grouse are restricted to those areas of the West where sagebrush grows extensively. A divergent species closely related to the blue grouse of coniferous forests, sage grouse occupy a unique niche within the sagebrush environment. A bird of huge proportions, the male sage grouse exceeds six pounds in weight. As one might imagine, only the most skillful and determined falcons are a match for such quarry.

As a group, prairie grouse are incompatible with modern agricultural practices. These practices have caused their ranges to shrink drastically in recent years. The remaining grouse are essentially remnant populations from the great days of expansive prairies, most of which fell to the plow and "progress" decades ago. However, viable populations of these birds still exist here and there across the plains of the U.S. and Canada. They are widely considered the ultimate challenge for those who strive for perfection in falconry.

In recent years, many different types of falcons have killed grouse. However, many of these grouse have been killed in poor style and in flights that could only loosely be called sporting. Young sage grouse (birds of the year) are slow targets and few game birds are easier to kill with a falcon. Molting adults are only slightly more difficult. These grouse have neither the strength nor stamina to fly far in the scorching heat of late summer and they are naively approachable at critical watering areas. While ideal quarry for entering and training eyasses, they represent no accomplishment for a well-trained falcon. Many grouse hawking aficionados hold off their campaigns until the weather cools in October. By then, the young grouse have matured and the older ones have gained the physical conditioning to flush explosively and leave the country: attributes that earned the species true trophy status.

What makes grouse hawking so addictive is the extreme difficulty of achieving quality kills by trained falcons. The terrain is rough, the weather cold and windy, and the speed of the grouse permits them to simply outfly most falcons at will. This is particularly true if the falcon is accustomed to coming up behind its quarry and "scooping" it up, which is an effective means of capturing most game. Grouse take the opportunity to barrel roll at just the right moment, to brush off the stoop, and then hyper-accelerate and outdistance the falcon. At that point, the average prairie falcon or peregrine gives up and mounts for another try.

On the other hand, gyrfalcons often take chase and may fly for miles across the plains in hot pursuit. If the gyr eventually catches the grouse, the falconer has no small task in finding and recovering the falcon.

Grouse have amazing physical strength. It is an incredible experience to see a large falcon stoop from a high pitch and knock down a grouse with the force of a falling piano, only to have the grouse bounce off the ground and fly out of sight. The grouse's back is like a plate of steel, so that a falcon has to hit the upper half of the body hard enough to break a wing or stun the grouse to stop it. No other game bird is equal to the grouse. Unfortunately, few falconers live in areas where they have easy access to such hawking.

PHEASANT

The ring-necked pheasant is probably the upland game bird most sought-after by North American falconers. Pheasants do not range into the southeastern U.S., but are plentiful throughout the Midwest, plains, and intermountain West. The species adapts well to modern agriculture, particularly where crops are irrigated. Because it frequents open grain fields, the pheasant may be hawked in classical style with falcons.

Despite its size, the pheasant is not particularly swift or maneuverable, but makes up for these shortcomings with cunning. In fact, there are times when a pheasant may drive a falconer to distraction with its sneaky ways. Unlike most upland game birds that freeze when a falcon is overhead, pheasants run like rabbits through the brush. Occasionally, they may run right out from under a point, scoot as fast as they can until they are out of cover, and then take to the air. If the falcon takes its time to leave the fist and mount to a high pitch, the point may be only a fond memory by the time the falconer is ready to flush. When this happens, the chase begins all over again. The falconer must attempt to have the dog point the pheasant without getting close enough to bump it, while trusting the falcon to stay overhead until the game appears. One may often have fine classic flights when pheasants hold for a pointer.

Until a falcon has killed a number of pheasants, the falconer will want to fly small groups in low cover and avoid the huge flocks that feed in the open fields. Large groups are too confusing for young falcons. Some pheasants in large groups will run in the open, some will fly directly from the cover, and others will fly a short distance, then drop back into cover. Rarely will they hold where expected. More often than not, a pheasant will tempt the falcon to engage in a tailchase instead of stooping from a decent pitch.

Ditches and hedgerows are difficult areas in which to hawk pheasants due to the extensive tracts of vegetation that enable the pheasant to run undetected instead of holding or flushing into the open. With two or more people, these escape corridors may be blocked before the falcon is released, thus forcing the pheasant to flush at the desired time. A dog that will head into cover and ferret out pheasants is also of great benefit. Like most game birds, pheasants occasionally will allow a person to walk right past them without flushing.

The unpredictable nature of the pheasant makes it a challenging quarry for a variety of medium-sized and large falcons. When hawked in sparse or isolated cover, pheasants do become more manageable. While falconers disagree about the merits of the ring-necked pheasant as a game bird, few dispute that it is a gourmet's delight.

PARTRIDGE

Partridge are intermediate-sized game birds that prefer open spaces. They are perfectly suited to work with a pointing dog, hold solidly with a falcon overhead, and race away from the area at high speed when flushed. These characteristics, and their compact size, make them challenging quarry for both falcons and tiercels. The two commonly hunted partridge species in North America are the Hungarian or gray partridge and the chukar partridge.

Hungarian partridge occupy diverse habitats across the continent. But "Huns" are best known for their preference for cereal grains. The greatest populations of Huns are found in the dryland wheat-producing regions in the northern states west of the Great Lakes and the southern regions of bordering Canadian provinces. There, Huns inhabit the open tracts of stubble and scab land that provide essential food and breeding grounds. Because these birds are nonmigratory, their populations fluctuate greatly with the weather in any given year. Huns seem better able to cope with prolonged cold weather than pheasants. This is due, in part, to their habit of burrowing down through snow to reach grain or green vegetation lying underneath. Coveys of Huns often make large "dugouts" in the snow in order to feed.

Huns are honest game birds and hold well for a pointer. However, if the birds are being shot at during the hunting season, they will begin flushing wild as the season progresses. This isn't as challenging for the falconer as for the gunner, for Huns generally hold well for a dog, but flush when the human form comes near. With a falcon in the air, partridge will freeze to the ground in terror. Unlike pheasants, which hit the ground running, a covey of flushed partridge will generally sit close to wherever they land, especially if the falcon is released quickly after they touch down. Thus, it is possible to hawk Huns in absolutely barren ground.

In some areas, such as the Palouse Hills of eastern Washington, Huns have radically altered their habits. Huns now rest and feed on chiseled ground devoid of cover, where they can detect predators coming from great distances. Such behavior provides no opportunity for a gun hunter to get close, but is an ideal situation for falconry. As Les Boyd of Pullman, Washington has ably demonstrated, the falconer must adapt to the changes in hawking conditions. Instead of walking for miles in the rolling hills behind his dogs, Les now drives the roads slowly, stopping frequently to "glass" the many hillsides with high-powered binoculars. Knowing the quarry's habits and the lay of the land is vital. As the late Dennis Cancellare once noted, "Les has the dirt clods numbered!" With his knowledge of partridge biology and his uncanny ability to spot these well-camouflaged birds under all weather conditions, he has developed partridge hawking to a fine art.

Coveys of partridge remain in the same immediate area year-round. The studies I have read suggest that partridge move less than a mile annually, but this probably depends on the quality of the local habitat. I have found coveys in nearly the same area time after time.

Hawking Huns in open stubble is great sport. They hold well as a rule, flush perfectly time after time, and fly explosively. For the best flights, partridge should be hawked away from cover. Anyone who has hawked winter Huns knows that the birds are determined flyers and are tough enough to withstand serious blows from a falcon and keep on going. Huns are about the size of a homing pigeon. In deep snow, these birds may be spotted in their "dugouts" and flown without the aid of a dog. Huns do have the habit, however, of diving out of the air and disappearing into the snow just when a falcon is about to close with them.

In contrast, chukar partridge occupy the up-and-down canyon country of the arid West and rarely may be found in areas suitable for hawking with longwings. Chukars lack the sustained flying power of Hungarian partridge and instead use steep, often mountainous, terrain for survival. In their element, chukars run uphill and fly downhill at great speed. It is more the use of its habitat, and not the excessive physical prowess of the chukar, which makes hawking them such a challenge.

Winter chukars gather in large flocks, sometimes in excess of thirty birds. They hold well to point and prefer to flush as singles or in small groups. Although half again bigger than a Hungarian partridge, they seem more intimidated by the falcon and less inclined to leave at full throttle on the reflush. If put in to thick cover such as sagebrush, they may refuse to flush altogether. They are also known to hide in rock piles and dive down badger holes to escape capture.

Throughout the Northwest, chukars and Huns occupy transitional zones together. In steeper grasslands and along rocky ridge tops one may encounter both species in terrain that is marginally suitable for hawking. The real key is a reliable hawking team. One needs a rock-solid pointer to provide the necessary slip. The falcon must mount to a high pitch without wandering. This is sport for falconers with stout legs and good lungs. It is inherently dangerous in that the terrain is not negotiable by road and the flights often carry the falcon and quarry great distances away downhill at top speed. Therefore, all necessary equipment such as telemetry, binoculars, and water must be packed during the hunt.

In the last three years, I have occasionally gone in pursuit of chukars with my red-naped shaheen, and a wide-ranging English Pointer. While I have not had the wherewithal to fully understand and master this branch of falconry, the team has enjoyed some success in bringing chukars to bag. At this point, I feel that I have learned more about chukar hawking than I have actually accomplished. However, this information may be useful to others who are also experimenting with chukars as longwing quarry.

CHUKAR PARTRIDGE

Attempting to fly falcons off mountain sides has its own inherent set of problems, not the least of which is getting into good chukar partridge habitat on foot. As in most forms of longwing hawking, choosing the proper terrain that optimizes your chances for a flight while minimizing the risk of losing your bird cannot be overemphasized. I have learned the hard way to avoid slopes with stands of sagebrush in preference for rocky or grassy inclines. My observation is that for a successful flight, the chukar must stay airborne for quite a long time. There are two reasons this is necessary. The first is that the partridge must bypass cover and try to escape by flying, not hiding. In what would be considered good hawking terrain, they have little choice but to do this anyway. The second is that in order for a trained falcon to catch a partridge that is driving headlong downhill like a feathered bullet, it needs time to accelerate to its terminal velocity. Because of the falcon's superior aerodynamic design (higher top-end speed and less air drag), it will eventually overtake the partridge in flight. However, the falcon requires a lot of room, vertical distance, in which to stoop and overtake the partridge. Time and distance, therefore, are integral parts of a successful slip on chukars.

Chukars have been killed by peregrines, shaheens, and prairie falcons, as well as prairie/peregrine and gyr/peregrine hybrids. One might imagine that the shape and speed of a hybrid tiercel displaying gyrfalcon characteristics could be put to good use in chukar hawking. Whatever the falcon of choice might be, it must take a high pitch and show patience. To quantify, I would say that the ideal falcon would wait-on at a pitch in excess of 1,500 feet and be willing to stay in position for at least an hour. During the course of a flight, the falcon may stoop completely out of sight, below the falconer, and be required to make its way up to the falconer's location from the bottom of a canyon more than half a mile away.

As demanding as the falcon's job is, the pivotal player in this form of hawking is the pointing dog. It probably takes a world-class pointer to do this correctly. A good pointer will cover steep, rocky ground at full speed and hold a point on birds almost indefinitely. Simply keeping up with a big running dog in up-and-down country is difficult, and I routinely put telemetry on my pointer. Because of the range at which they work, the dog may be lost to sight when it locates a covey. A dog on point in some deep, hidden draw is easy to overlook. Such opportunities are wasted unless you have some communication link with the dog that allows you to capitalize on the situation.

While most dogs are good at tracking you down after a long run, there are times when you can, and will, lose such a dog in a remote area. The basic purpose of telemetry is that it can ensure that you spend more time looking for game than you do for your dog or hawk.

My sorties into chukar country lead me to the conclusion that this branch of the falconer's art offers one of the greatest challenges currently available in North American game hawking. Through chukar hawking (and other forms of falconry), we have the opportunity to apply current falcon training techniques and use modern equipment in a manner that both extends and expands the sport of falconry beyond its historic paradigms.

STRATEGIES FOR UPLAND GAME

The basic techniques for flushing game have been discussed in previous chapters. But unlike duck hawking, where the falcon can actually see game prior to the flush, an upland game hawk must trust the team below to produce hunting opportunities from a seemingly barren landscape. Only a consistent supply of quality slips at wild quarry perpetuates high-caliber game hawking.

A good dog will find birds if the ground is adequately populated. However, this generally means miles of time-consuming leg work for both dog and falconer. If one is pressed for time, as when hawking in the last hour or two of the day after work, cruising the roads for exposed birds may prove expedient. During mornings and evenings, upland game birds feed in low stubble or mill around roadbanks to pick up gravel, which aids digestion. Edges of grain fields that lie adjacent to grazing land or thick brush may also be productive. Often, bumping a covey off the roadbank makes for a good marked flight. Ideally, the falconer has a dog on point and then puts up the falcon. But when hunting marked coveys or flocks, especially pheasants, one wants to get the falcon up as soon as possible to keep the game from fleeing, and then move in with the dog for a close, accurate point. The game already has been alerted that trouble is coming, so the element of surprise is somewhat diluted. One may also drive back roads or along cut grainfields while allowing pointers to search the ground parallel to the vehicle.

During midday, game may be harder to find, as the birds rest in heavy cover. They seek such areas for shade in hot weather and wind breaks when it is cold. Standing crops, such as field corn, often serve this dual purpose. I have found it necessary to run a dog in likely looking cover and either fly a point or bump the birds in hopes of getting them into sparser cover where they have less advantage.

In desert country, game is concentrated at water holes or succulent vegetation early in the season. The falconer may examine the edge of the water course for footprints, feathers, and droppings. One may then scout the surrounding area for game or wait until dawn or dusk for the birds to come for water. Desert quail can never be far from their drinking water; by walking the creeks or draws in the immediate vicinity, one may locate coveys. Also, "sign" of large birds, such as sage grouse, is particularly obvious at the cattle tanks in open range country.

Prairie chickens are known to frequent certain areas at particular times of the day. Once these areas are discovered, the falconer may simply arrive at the appropriate time and mark the birds when they come in to feed. The falcon is released while the dog works in for a point and a flush is produced.

In colder climates, upland game hawking techniques change in response to the severity of the winter and the depth of snow. For instance, pheasants in deep snow often flush wild in the open at great distances, and may not hold if a falconer enters the field a half mile away. Neither falconer nor dog can catch up to a pheasant in a foot race under such conditions. Conversely, pheasants may allow themselves to be solidly pinned down when they bunch into cover or standing grain crops. These islands of feed and cover are often surrounded by fields of snow, making for dramatic flights. In addition, it may be possible to track pheasants in snow and produce a flight.

While deep snow is a hindrance to pheasant hawking, it can actually enhance partridge hawking. Because they are so nondescript in appearance, these birds are difficult to spot during most of the year. With a blanket of snow on the ground, their open-country habits help to make them more visible to falconers. Often in winter, a covey will reside near a shelter belt, farm house, or hedgerow for feed and cover. It may be necessary to intentionally flush these birds away from such refuge before attempting to hawk them. Sometimes, it is advantageous to bump a covey into light cover to ensure that they hold satisfactorily when the falcon is released. Hungarian partridge tend to sit tighter and let the falconer get closer to them if they are hidden in a thick bush. Heavy snow with a thick crust makes upland game vulnerable to predators. Under these conditions, they become jumpy and difficult to approach.

During gunning season, one must be aware that game birds will be more alert and defensive. In my area, most of the fields are plowed in early fall and pheasants hide in the standing corn for protection. In uncut corn, they are essentially safe from a falcon. But on days when mobs of shooters drive the fields, pheasants may be found standing *en masse* in the middle of barren, plowed ground, a situation that may be quite advantageous for the falconer.

The knack of "reading" ground cover is one that comes through study, field experience, and trial and error. The successful falconer learns to identify the cover (crops, pastures, ditches, trees, brush piles, plowed fields, etc.) used by different quarry. In many instances, a cover type or a mosaic of cover types may suggest an abundance of a particular species of upland game bird. The habits of a game bird within its environment must be learned in order to predict, with any degree of accuracy, what its response will be when being chased by a falcon. Once one knows and can anticipate a quarry's escape maneuvers, these actions can be countered in an effort to give the falcon an advantage. Conversely, it is just as important to know what cover types work against a falcon in a hunting situation and should be avoided.

This lesson was driven home to me during a hawking trip to South Dakota with my lifelong friend, Brad Mitchell. The quarry was Hungarian partridge, the same game bird that I hawk at home in Idaho. I was to learn the hard way, however, that there were some regional differences influencing this quarry's behavior. Near my home, coveys of partridge can be scarce. Finding them is often time consuming, involving a lot of walking. Where I find them, the cover is sparse and almost every mark or point is worth flying. These partridge generally fly completely out of sight after being flushed, so each slip is a one-time opportunity. The situation on the northern plains was somewhat different. Huns were available in greater numbers that allowed us to drive the roads and locate coveys. I was very excited at the hawking prospects and, at first, found it difficult to drive past coveys of partridge sitting conspicuously in the open between the rows of corn stalks. On more than one occasion, zeal for a flight threatened to overcome good judgment. Fortunately, Brad was quick to remind me that seeing quarry did not, in itself, constitute a slip. Brad's experience was that Huns headed straight for standing corn and chest-high grass when flushed; they also dove repeatedly into cover if reflushed. It was, therefore, up to us to find partridge far from cover, in areas where they were forced to fly long distances to reach sanctuary. After suffering the repercussions of a poorly chosen slip (high pitch and valuable time wasted, disappointed falcon and a surly companion), the merits of slip analysis were driven home.

14 Captive Breeding

Captive breeding of birds of prey, a technology developed in the last twenty years, stands as a lasting legacy for future generations of falconers. This avicultural endeavor has fallen almost solely to the falconry community. Current information on nutrition, breeding behavior, facilities, breeding stock management, and incubation techniques applicable to raptors is directly attributable to the efforts of falconers, as is the survival and recovery of peregrine falcons in North America. Today, this information has international applications to both falconry and propagators working to recover threatened and endangered raptor populations.

The most conspicuous element, the common thread, that has bound these innovative falconer/breeders together is an appreciation for individual birds of prey. The intimate relationships of falconer/breeders with their birds and their understanding of falcons, in particular, led them to the creation of a captive propagation technology that was, up until the early 1970s, unknown for the previous 4,000 years that man and raptors have been associated. Largely the result of convergent thinking and experimentation by falconers across the continent, techniques for the captive breeding of raptors gradually began to surface. A core of farsighted falconers helped launch The Peregrine Fund specifically to propagate peregrine falcons for reintroduction purposes. Other falconers supported this effort financially, politically, and logistically. The free and open exchange of ideas, fostered by North American raptor breeders who put the welfare of the birds ahead of personal gain, stands in stark contrast to other parts of the world where this information has been jealously guarded.

There is now linkage between the captive breeding of raptors in North America and the credibility of falconers. Many of the more desirable raptors, from a falconer's perspective, are rare, endangered, or politically sensitive. Today, the majority of large falcons being flown for falconry come from private breeding establishments. Many falconer/breeders specialize in the production of certain species, subspecies, or hybrids. Personal tastes, more than anything else, will dictate what types of falcons are maintained in the breeding chambers of the future. Private breeders, keeping limited numbers of birds that can be sold at fair market prices, have shown how captive breeding can be carried on in an efficient and cost-effective manner. In addition to being the sole source of many hybrid, rare, or exotic raptors for falconry, private breeders now supply a significant number of peregrine falcons for reintroduction efforts.

In the western U.S. and Canada, the endangered anatum subspecies of the peregrine falcon has been reestablished throughout most of its former range. Areas of the Southwest are known to have viable populations that may soon be downlisted from their endangered status. Public and government support for some endangered species programs is diminishing. Money once spent on single, high-profile species is now being focused on holistic, ecosystem programs. As peregrine reintroduction nears its conclusion, large, institutional breeding establishments may prove to be economically unfeasible. It would, unfortunately, be naive to assume that peregrine populations will not benefit from, or require, continued, low-level augmentation in certain locales. The anatum peregrine and its prey still suffer in some areas from the effects of pesticide contamination. However, breeding pairs of anatum peregrines, representing a diverse gene pool, could be held among private breeders to maintain an affordable alternative for long-term, low-level population augmentation. Governments might also encourage falconers to fly, breed, and, eventually, release anatum peregrines into the wild as yet another means of assisting anatum peregrine populations at no cost to the taxpayers.

It behooves falconers to remain conscious of their reputation. While it is difficult to erase some people's negative opinions of hunting, predators, and keeping wild animals in captivity, we must always strive to put forth a flattering image of ourselves. The image of a group that gives something back to the resources it uses, or that actually saved a favored resource from extinction, is extremely positive. The captive breeding of raptors for falconry and for the continued benefit of wild populations of raptors, wherever they may be, is apt to be one of our greatest image enhancers.

Widely accepted as the raptor breeder's bible, *Falcon Propagation: A Manual On Captive Breeding,* is a collection of information contributed by many experts. The manual describes propagation techniques for captive raptors that were developed from the late 1960s to the early 1980s. It also offers important management and maintenance suggestions to help the raptor breeder solve the ongoing problems inherent in this endeavor. Since its publication, additional information and experimentation have developed that further our general knowledge about captive breeding. The average North American falconer can now purchase captive-bred peregrines, for example, at an affordable price. At present, it is cheaper to buy falcons than raise them. However, I believe the small-scale captive production of raptors will continue, given a certain set of criteria. First, I assume that after being denied access to peregrines and other desirable species for so long, many falconers want to ensure that they always have access to, and a choice of, the kinds of birds they prefer. Many falconers also enjoy the husbandry aspect of raising birds. Considering that one good pair of birds can produce an average of five or six young each year, I foresee more cooperatives being formed among falconers to maintain breeding pairs. It is, after all, the rearing or acquisition of the hawk food, and not the raising of the hawks, that requires the greatest time commitment on the part of the breeder. If people share the work, they can also expect to share the wealth, so to speak.

The reader of the classic works of falconry need not search far to detect a historical bias directed at eyas falcons. Edmund Bert wrote, "The eyass, upon whom I can fasten no affection." And Simon Latham offered: "But leaving to speak any more of these scratching kind of hawks, that I never did love should come to neare my fingers..." An important accomplishment of North American falconers, and a prime motivator for continued interest in captive breeding, has been the true mastery of the eyas falcon. Exemplary falconer/breeders, like Jim Weaver and Les Boyd, not only produced and flew their own captive-bred falcons, but took game hawking to new levels of excellence with these "homegrown" hawks. The real, hard-core grouse hawking in North America was pioneered, for all intents and purposes, with captive-bred eyas falcons.

The personal relationship that one may develop with an eyas falcon is special. And, of course, it helps to know that the falcon can be just as wonderful in the air as it is at home on the block.

BREEDING STOCK SELECTION

I have little practical experience in breeding imprints. But I do know that pairs of falcons that copulate, incubate, and feed young are easy to maintain. These "natural" breeding pairs will save the breeder untold hours that might otherwise be diverted from work, family, or other interests. For that reason, I will direct my comments toward this group.

A lot of resources have been wasted on efforts to breed falcons that never produced young. There are some examples of birds breeding after being re-paired or relocated in different facilities, but the odds are against this. Falcons destined to be natural breeders must have the proper mental image to recognize themselves as birds. They must also be at ease with their surroundings. A bird that is constantly being upset by disturbances in or around the chamber building, or a bird that is too nervous to court its mate properly, should be considered a poor candidate and replaced.

Falconry birds often make the best breeders. Their daily association with man and his activities predisposes them to ignore a variety of potential disruptions. For that reason, I suggest that the aspiring breeder consider incorporating intermewed game hawks as breeders. When making a financial investment in breeding stock, however, it is important to weigh the potential gains made by flying a bird against the real possibility that the bird could be killed or lost. No bird that is irreplaceable should ever be put at risk in the field.

Potential breeding stock should be carefully screened. Hard-earned experience has taught me that it is important to know the intimate history of each bird: its lineage, its diet, the way it was reared, fledged, handled and flown, and its falconry performance. Only with accurate information can a proper assessment be made regarding a particular bird's suitability for breeding.

Birds that will not be flown for falconry should be handled, blocked out during the day, and exposed to the mainstream of household activities. At The Peregrine Fund, eyasses taken from chambers before they fledge are jessed and blocked in a well-attended weathering yard where they see people all day long. While they are not fed on the fist or handled individually, this process acclimates the birds to their surroundings. As a rule, these eyasses are paired and placed in chambers during late fall.

Eyasses that I have held back for breeding fit into three different categories. One group was raised as a cohort in a hack box, fledged in a large chamber, and taken up at approximately sixty-five days of age. A second group was simply left with the parents for about the same period of time. The cohort-reared group manned very quickly and seemed particularly easy going. Eyasses reared by parents were wilder, took longer to man, and were never as calm as the cohort-raised group. To counteract the behavior of the parent-raised group, I handled them for one year before putting them in chambers. The third group of falcons was reared with other eyasses, then hacked and flown as a cast for several months before being put up. They were handled like imprints but always kept together. Birds in this category are sometimes referred to as "dual socialized." Like imprints, they showed no fear of their surroundings or inhibitions around people and adapted well to chamber life. I am aware of many eyasses raised in such a manner that have become prolific natural breeders.

Based on my limited experiences and personal preferences, I would rank the cohort-reared eyasses as the first choice. They required the shortest investment of time and the least amount of work on my part. The dual-socialized eyasses were great fun but, similar to imprints, they were extremely labor intensive and for this reason alone, I would rate them second. Parent-reared eyasses appeal to a number of falconers who believe that such birds have the mentality most like wild-taken birds. If left much after fledging age (45-days old), they can be indeed wild, but in all the wrong ways. To truly enhance the breeding opportunities from parent-reared eyasses that are left in chambers past hard penning, they should be flown hard for two seasons before being consigned to the breeding program.

INCUBATION

There is overwhelming evidence to suggest that falcon eggs are more likely to hatch if they receive some natural incubation under falcons or setting chickens initially. While they can be left longer, a period from five to ten days is considered adequate. Pulling clutches of eggs after this limited period of time permits the breeder to maximize production by encouraging second clutches from pairs. It also allows the breeder to manipulate problem eggs or assist problem chicks that might not otherwise hatch.

Most breeders artificially incubate eggs according to The Peregrine Fund guidelines with Roll-X incubators equipped with automatic egg-turning grids. This method requires the use of three incubators set at 99.5° F (37.5° C). The goal is for each egg to lose approximately 15 percent of its fresh weight, determined on the day it was laid, over a 32-day period. Eggs begin incubation at a set level of humidity and are weighed every three days. If the egg loses too much weight, it is placed in an incubator with higher humidity (more surface area of water). If the egg is not losing enough weight, it goes into a dry incubator.

The incubation technique that I use, with good results, is somewhat different. Developed and recommended to me by Les Boyd, this method involves the misting of eggs five times every twenty-four hours. I use a plastic "plant sprayer" bottle with either deionized or distilled water kept at room temperature. Because of the frequent intervals at which the incubator lid is raised and the eggs are misted, I also hand-turn the eggs: use of the automatic turner is optional. Opening an incubator is known to cause a temporary increase in temperature and loss of humidity, but this seems to be offset by the misting procedure.

The "turn and spray" technique has been used successfully to hatch peregrine and prairie/peregrine hybrid eggs that had no natural incubation. There is evidence to suggest that eggs should be turned more frequently at the start of incubation. To compensate for a lack of natural incubation, some breeders will turn and spray eggs every three hours around the clock for the first two weeks of incubation. Eggs incubated in this fashion are known to hatch at extreme variations in weight loss. Although this is a demanding method of incubation for a short period of time, it is an alternative to purchasing additional incubators and caring for setting chickens.

Within a constant incubation environment, the porosity of the eggs of various raptors affects their respective rate of weight loss. Therefore, breeders must experiment with the level of humidity used in an incubator for each species. For instance, I incubated a clutch of prairie falcon eggs, from day one with no natural incubation, in a dry incubator. They tracked the 15 percent weight loss perfectly. However, it was necessary to fill one quadrant of my Roll-X with water to prevent excessive weight loss in a clutch of peregrine eggs in the same incubator. We know that some species, like prairie falcons, are tolerant of incubation extremes; these same eggs may have hatched perfectly well in a more humid incubator. It is, however, important for breeders to recognize these differences and apply tighter incubation tolerances to the more demanding species.

DIET

If grown and maintained on a nutritionally well-balanced feed, a single, production-line food package, like Coturnix quail, is an adequate diet for maintaining most raptors. However, the small raptor breeder can do much to ensure the continued good health of adults, and increase the quality of eggs and chicks produced, by varying the diet of captive breeding stock. Over the course of a year, I feed a mixture of Coturnix quail, chicken, pigeon (carefully cleaned and frozen), house sparrows, and game birds. That captive raptors need nutritional variety is, to me, common sense.

Some food items may not be appropriate or safe for certain species of raptors. For example, pigeons are known carriers of many diseases harmful to raptors and even people. In certain places, they carry a herpes virus that is particularly devastating to gyrfalcons. Yet, peregrines around the world eat pigeons and doves.

I believe the key is careful inspection and processing of the food offered to captive stock. The small breeding project has certain advantages. Foremost among them is that a high degree of quality control in feeding can be maintained. The small-scale raptor breeder has the luxury of an intimate awareness of the health and behavior of individual birds. If there is a problem, it can be detected and solved promptly.

THE "K-PAD" BROODING METHOD

The K-pad is an automated hot water bottle. An electrical pump sends warmed water throughout the pad, via a network

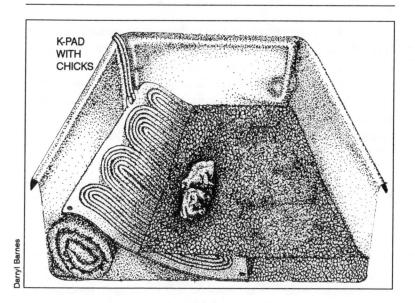

of tubes, creating a mat of constant, adjustable heat. Used mostly in hospitals, K-pads may be purchased from medical supply houses. I have found this to be both the easiest and best means of brooding chicks for their first ten days of life.

One way to use the K-pad is described and illustrated in *Falcon Propagation.* I put the K-pad inside a large tub or the shell of older-style human baby incubator to prevent drafts. By draping the K-pad over a rolled up towel, I create a roll or hump on one side. I cover the K-pad with a pillow case or thin towel, mostly to keep it clean, then line the floor area with about one inch of well-washed pea gravel. The inclining angle of the K-pad has two functions; it gives the chick something to lean against and, because the gravel is shallower near the pad, the chick can get warmer or cooler by simply shifting its body one way or the other. Where the K-pad and the pea gravel come together, a cup-like depression is made and the chicks are placed in it. The depression keeps the chick next to the heat, and directs its legs underneath its body. I have had no problem with falcon chicks developing splayed legs—a physical deformity caused by a smooth or soft substrate that furnishes poor footing.

As soon as the newly hatched chick is inspected, weighed, and has had its navel swabbed with iodine, I put it on the K-pad. Early on, I left chicks in a hatcher for about eight hours or roughly until the first feeding. I learned that if the chick is put on the K-pad and covered loosely with a folded towel, it drys and fluffs out very quickly. It is also important to remove newly hatched chicks from a humid incubator environment that can contribute to respiratory ailments.

CHAMBER DESIGN

Falcons have bred in chambers of diverse sizes and designs, some of palatial proportions and others little more than glorified toolsheds. It may be true, to some extent, that the right pair of falcons will breed in any size structure. But it is equally true that a properly designed chamber will encourage breeding by enhancing, or perhaps not inhibiting, these natural tendencies. The optimum size for a universal breeding chamber, one that accommodates the largest number of raptor species properly, has yet to be determined. Based on successes, however, we do know that all species of large falcons will breed in a chamber 10-feet wide, 20-feet long, and 12-feet high. Personally, I would not want to test pairs in chambers less than 10-feet high or 16-feet long.

My chambers are modeled, more or less, after The Peregrine Fund design. They include an antechamber that serves as a safety entrance. A nest ledge, located high on the wall and equipped with access doors, runs the full width of the chamber. These chambers are designed to allow easy viewing of, and prompt access to, the nest ledge. It is extremely practical for taking eggs and manipulating chicks among pairs.

However, another chamber style, developed by Les Boyd and widely copied here in the Northwest, has proven to be successful. Somewhat less expensive than a comparably sized structure built of plywood and two-by-fours, Les advocates a pole barn structure of vertical, rough-cut planks (1 inch by 12 inches). The roof is mostly cyclone fence with solid roof coverings at each end of the chambers for protection from the elements. A covered nest box (2-feet wide, 4-feet long, and 3-feet high) is attached at the midpoint along one of the long walls. The bottom of the nest box is about six feet above the floor. High and low perches are attached to opposite ends of the chamber.

This chamber style offers advantages that are somewhat different from those of The Peregrine Fund design. First, it is less expensive and relatively easy to construct. The open top allows considerable sunlight, which is good for the birds and helps to disinfect the chamber interior. According to Les, this design has the further advantage of encouraging the tiercel to do "fly bys" over the head of the female, an essential part of courtship behavior. In his chambers, even wild-caught Barbary falcons have bred.

I concur with the general consensus that cocomat perches are beneficial for falcons confined to chambers. Considering the heightened level of activity displayed by courting falcons each spring, and the considerable bouncing around that they do, I think it wise to have perches that help absorb the shock of a bird landing hard. I am also a proponent of open roofs incorporating either metal conduit or rounded 1-inch by 2-inch slats. Many falcons panic when people enter their chambers. A well-designed roof can help prevent superficial damage to their cere and plumage and also discourage falcons from hitting themselves hard enough to do serious injury.

PAIR MANAGEMENT

The goal of my system for selecting, housing, feeding, and caring for potential breeding stock is the establishment of a productive pair of falcons. The system is also designed to have the falcons do the most critical and the most tedious tasks associated with falcon production.

Eggs don't hatch unless they are fertile. A good pair of falcons will court and copulate, with the net result that most eggs laid will be fertile. Anyone who has artificially inseminated falcons can testify to the true value of a compatible pair in terms of work reduction for the falconer/breeder and minimized disruption of the falcon pair. While other falconer/breeders are collecting semen from tiercels, netting and everting laying falcons, or, perhaps, courting imprint falcons several times daily, the owner of an established pair of natural breeders has little to do but casually observe the courting and incubating behavior of the pair.

As they mature, a pair of falcons must progress along a series of steps on the road to successful breeding. Behavioral changes in the pair, triggered by sexual hormones, are dramatic. Though both birds are normally solitary and standoffish, the ritualized feedings of the falcon by the tiercel strengthen their bonds; the birds sit next to each other and generally do things in a more intimate way. As the falcon begins laying, the attention of the pair is focused on the scrape. As she nears completion of the clutch, they begin the shared duty of incubation. There is probably nothing more important in the natural progression of a pair bond than for the male and female to both participate in incubation. For new pairs, and especially for first-time, egg-laying females, this is a critical stage, often a "make or break" point in their development as breeders.

Cooperative incubation is mandatory because without the hormonal surge associated with this activity, pairs cannot be trusted to feed eyasses. At some point after the pair has been incubating for between two and four weeks, they must be tested as parents. Many falconer/breeders believe that if pairs are to become effective copulators and dependable eyas feeders, they must begin learning these skills early in life. Therefore, all efforts should be made to obtain an eyas or, preferably, a brood of two to four eyasses that are less than ten days of age. The visual stimulation of a group of eyasses, and the chatter associated with food begging, work together to bring about the desired response of the adults. The species of falcon used for this experiment is of no consequence. Even eyas kestrels can be well cared for by the larger species of falcons. The important factor is for the eyasses to be young enough to require brooding by the adults for several days. Would-be parents must satisfy this need to brood. Older eyasses sometimes put themselves at risk by objecting to the advances of the adults.

Falcons have been hatching their own eggs for eons, and some falconer/breeders believe that pairs laying for the first time should be left to hatch out their first clutch of eggs. There are certainly some advantages to allowing falcons to experience full-term incubation and the parent-offspring bonding that takes place when chicks hatch. However, there is always the risk that the first clutch of eggs left under the falcons will be infertile. One has the option of taking the clutch and replacing it with dummy eggs. The eggs may then be candled to determine fertility and returned to the pair at a later date if desired. For the falconer/breeder who only needs two or three eyasses annually, or who can't devote eight weeks each spring to incubating eggs and rearing eyasses, a pair that will raise its own young may be ideal.

Like a number of my colleagues, I'm still interested in maximizing my annual production of peregrines, but with a minimum of effort. My routine is to allow my older pairs to lay a clutch of eggs and incubate for ten days to provide the much-desired period of natural incubation. I then "recycle" the pair by removing the first clutch and placing these eggs in an incubator. Approximately fourteen days later, the female begins laying her second clutch of eggs. The first clutch of eggs is artificially incubated and the chicks that hatch are hand-fed for approximately ten days. By this time, the second clutch of eggs has been laid and naturally incubated, also for approximately ten days. I then take the second clutch of eggs and deposit the first group of chicks in their place on the nest ledge. The careful steps involved in exchanging young for eggs, which should be reviewed, are outlined in "Falcon Propagation." The parents thus take over the laborious chore of feeding the nearly insatiable young. By substituting younger groups of eyasses for older ones, an established pair can be trusted to feed several cohorts of young falcons over the course of the spring. After a pair has been feeding for several weeks, however, the adults lose their desire to brood chicks. In this case, eyasses given to adults must be over fourteen days of age and able to regulate their own body temperature.

One pair of breeding falcons qualifies as a hobby. But, as I have found, the demands created by two or more pairs dramatically change the complexion of even small-scale falcon breeding from fun to work. The management scheme applied to maturing pairs will, in all likelihood, determine their future role as breeders. One must, therefore, carefully weigh the desired capabilities and behavior of the pair against the falconer/breeder's investment of time and the need for production.

15 Epilogue

> Who is watching means nothing; the species of hawk means nothing. What really matters is the level of achievement that you set as a goal, and your personal appraisal of your ability to reach it.
>
> — *Charles H. Schwartz*

Today's falconers suffer from an ancient Chinese curse: we live in interesting times. As with yin and yang, there is no all black or all white. This curse is both a burden and a privilege.

In the spring of 1980, I visited the historic "Peregrine Palace" at Cornell University in New York. My purpose there was twofold. First, I wanted to see the incredible collection of falcons from around the world, the founding stock for much of today's captive breeding efforts. In addition, I wanted to meet Jim Weaver, manager of the mission to reintroduce captive-bred peregrine falcons into the eastern U.S. Surrounded by rows of courting falcon pairs and a thick blanket of snow, the conversation eventually turned to falconry. At the time, Jim made a statement that I didn't fully comprehend. He said, simply, "The best is yet to come." Looking back over the past ten years, I'd have to say he was right. The second Golden Age of falconry is clearly underway in North America.

Not long ago, falconry was described as a "sport under wraps." One might view any ancient art form, perpetuated by a tightly knit group of enthusiasts who guard their secrets closely, in such cryptic terms. Between 1920 and 1970, the founders of North American falconry had to contend with a zealous core of oologists (egg collectors) who annually stole entire clutches of the rarer falcon and hawk eggs to hoard in their extensive collections. During the same period, neither wild nor trained birds of prey were safe from shooters and pigeon fanciers who legally gunned down every raptor that came in range. Places like Hawk Mountain in Pennsylvania and Cape May, New Jersey, known worldwide today as premier hawk-watching locations, were once well-publicized places for the wholesale slaughter of migrating hawks. Even the coastal migration route of the tundra peregrine was discovered, in part, as the result of falcons killed by gunners. Another sign of the times was the almost universally held notion that all predators were bad.

Viewed in this light, the protective mind set of early-day North American falconers is easy to appreciate. Locations of raptor nests, as well as focal points for migrating birds of prey, became coveted secrets passed only from friend to trusted friend. Likewise, falconry arts and skills, information that in the wrong hands could be used to destroy birds of prey, were shrouded in secrecy. It was the considered opinion of most falconers of the day that the less the public knew about falconry, the better. A few even suggested that falconers who actually caught game with their birds would offend the public and cause the sport's demise.

Up until 1975, falconers were basically ignored by the natural resource agencies charged with wildlife management. Because falconry is a world unto itself, most outsiders have no concept of either what trained birds of prey can and can't do or how falconers conduct their activities. Widespread ignorance about falconry, coupled with the tight-lipped secrecy of the falconry community and a sudden international concern for the welfare of all birds of prey, created a climate of misunderstandings and misconceptions that, on occasion, discredited the falconry community. It was often unclear through the media that peregrine falcon populations had become endangered as the

PEREGRINE HEAD STUDY

Darryl Barnes

result of pesticide contamination, not by the actions of falconers. Because certain agency officials and influential citizens knew nothing about the activities of falconers, they suspected the worst. That their suspicions had no basis didn't divert them from attempting to defame the practice of falconry.

In retrospect, it was the peregrine and its eminent danger of extinction that brought falconers and their unique knowledge of bird biology and behavior into the public eye. The early 1970s marked a new period of environmental awareness. At the forefront of the ecological movement, and one of its most dramatic symbols, was the peregrine falcon. As Tom Cade pointed out in his masterful work, *The Falcons of the World,* the plight of the peregrine falcon was brought to the world's attention by falconers, many of whom were professional biologists. Captive breeding techniques for falcons and other raptors were developed solely by falconers. The "hacking" method for releasing young captive-bred falcons to the wild is a falconry derivative, and continued population monitoring is being conducted, in large part, by falconers. It is no accident that the reestablishment of peregrine falcon populations in North America is considered one of the most sophisticated and successful wildlife recovery efforts of all time.

Over the past twenty years, falconry has endured tremendous change. Information on many relevant topics can now be found in the burgeoning body of falconry literature. Much of this exchange has been facilitated through publications of the North American Falconers Association. These publications feature the latest technical advances in equipment, medicine, training techniques, and raptor husbandry. Across the country, hunting laws have been created especially for falconry and, in some cases, greatly liberalized to allow falconers to take full advantage of extended seasons. Adequate, long-term exercise for captive raptors, allowing them to fulfill their natural role as predators, is encouraged by field seasons that span up to seven months in duration.

North American falconers are privy to sources of rare and unusual birds of prey through captive raptor propagation that was undreamed of two decades ago. In the past, a falconer desiring an eyas gyrfalcon, for example, had to mount an Arctic expedition to collect one. But today, birds of prey from around the world, as well as new combinations of hybrid falcons, are available from commercial sources. For those falconers willing to spend the money, rare hawks and falcons have never been easier to acquire.

The good things now possible for North American falconers come from the hard work of many people. The legitimization of the sport is largely the outcome of falconers banding together under the banner of the North American Falconers Association and responding in a highly professional manner to intense government scrutiny. To my knowledge, no other field sport in history has been subjected to the bureaucratic discrimination and regulatory restrictions directed at falconry in the United States since 1975. That falconry has survived recurring political maneuverings to outlaw the sport in this country is, in some ways, surprising. That it now reaches a heretofore unknown level of political success and respect is truly remarkable. The credibility of falconry has been established through publicly dispelling the unsubstantiated accusations of a few bigoted individuals. So far, scientific evidence supporting falconry has overcome the emotionally based criticism of its detractors. Campaigning against their political enemies has made falconers strong. Adversity has transformed a rather unlikely group of freewheeling sport hunters into a strong and effective political lobby; an odd but necessary metamorphosis.

One of my favorite falconry articles is "Life With An Indian Prince," written by Frank and John Craighead, the now world renowned wildlife researchers. Published in *The National Geographic Magazine* in 1942, it chronicled the adventures of two young American falconers who experienced the life of opulent Indian royalty and an intense, institutionalized pursuit of falconry that has since passed on to the realm of antiquity.

Their host, K. S. Dharmakumarsinhji, Bapa for short, literally had his pick of every type of fresh-trapped falcon native to the Indian subcontinent. Falconer/retainers trained them all *en masse* for diverse flights at a wide variety of quarry. What fascinated me was that despite all the peregrines, sakers, and shaheens on hand, Bapa's source of greatest pride was his lugger falcon. Widely disregarded by Indian falconers for their lackluster performance, Bapa had successfully groomed this small desert falcon for flights at partridge and ducks.

This story serves to illustrate one important point: a falconer's pride, self-worth, and sense of satisfaction depend largely on how he or she defines the challenge. That we cannot judge ourselves by the standards of turn-of-the-century British falconers, or even of 1960s North American falconers, is evident.

On the whole, we have fewer places to fly falcons and less game to pursue than we did thirty years ago. In contrast, we have access to a wider variety of falcons that are generally better trained and less likely to be lost. We also have longer hunting seasons in which to legally pursue quarry than at any time in the past. Our greatest obstacles are our expanding national population and "progress," which results in the wholesale loss of wildlife habitat and hunting areas.

Demographic projections for the U.S. suggest that by the year 2010, over 80 percent of the population will live in less than thirty major metropolitan areas. Most falconers will live near these population centers. After all, it was the creation of a well-paid working class, one that could afford the time and money for all-consuming pursuits like falconry, that has allowed the sport to persist and gain in popularity. The adaptation of falconers to the suburbs is evident across the country, and we can expect some novel approaches to develop in the future. That falconers in the heavily populated environs of New England are regularly catching ducks with large falcons on the coastal marshes is a fine testament to Yankee ingenuity. More and more, we should expect to hear of falconers taking advantage of nontraditional quarries as well as those familiar species, such as feral pigeons and starlings, that proliferate alongside man.

Techniques that allow familiar falcons to be flown in new ways, or perhaps various hybrid combinations groomed for specific quarry, are apt to find devotees among this new class of urban falconer. It will be necessary to keep an open mind and conduct field experiments before we can redefine what is, or can be, possible from a falconry perspective.

We have reached the point where it is logical to ask the question: what's next? For the past two decades, the numbers of practicing falconers have remained nearly constant but the sport has experienced an incredibly fertile period of technical advancement. The basics of falconry have, with minor alterations, remained unchanged for thousands of years. It is unlikely that further innovations as profound as captive breeding, telemetry, or modern medicines, will appear for many generations. One might effectively argue that falconry, like its symbol the peregrine, simply adapted to the changes brought on by the social consciousness and environmental disasters of this century. High-tech developments, including telemetry, were certainly timely creations well-adapted for the sport's benefit.

Peregrine falcons are no longer in danger of extinction on this continent. It is to the credit of the falconry community that it came to the aid of the peregrine at such a critical point in history. Of greater concern today is the land base supporting wild raptor populations and the space and game that allow the practice of falconry in its many forms. That much of the public and private land in this country has been mismanaged, and in some cases permanently damaged, for the benefit of commercial interests is fact. Falconers must, as a unit, bring pressure to bear on state and federal natural resource agencies to manage lands in the true spirit of conservation. In the case of private landholdings, there are limited means to affect compliance with government standards. However, falconers should strive to enhance the suitability of these lands for wildlife where appropriate, and work to ensure that they remain open for hunting. Depending on the location, purchasing and grooming a piece of ground (wildlife habitat) specifically for falconry may be a realistic alternative for some.

I have a charmed vision for the future of falconry in North America. It transcends mere pedantics and passive observation to include the challenges and satisfaction that can only come from hands-on experience. It is my opinion that falconry is a sport for stimulus addicts. To my knowledge, only dedicated falconers would ever give so much for so little. That falconry is a cerebral pursuit, much like chess, should be obvious. Like chess, the qualities of falconry can only be judged by an intangible set of criteria. In essence, today's falconers pit an ancient hunting art (albeit with the services of some modern conveniences) against the continual shock waves of an emerging technology and a rapidly altering landscape. That falconers are few is not important. That they are among life's activists is.

I keep asking myself what falconry challenges are left to experience in North America. What will be the "adventure" falconry for this decade and beyond? Topping the list for me, personally, would be the taking and training of large falcons from the wild. I can imagine few things as thrilling as rafting an Arctic river in search of gyrfalcons or roping down a high, storm-torn sea wall, overlooking the Pacific Ocean, to choose from a brood of hissing eyas Peale's falcons. At one time, beach trapping was an annual event for "regulars" who arrived at places like the old Coast Guard station on Assateague Island, Virginia, and the motels at Galveston and Corpus Christi, Texas. This brief, three-week window of opportunity every October was an autumnal vacation for many falconers, not unlike a field meet, where they gathered with old friends from around the country. The love of a trapping art they perfected, the rare pleasure of seeing many peregrines, and the rapture of fulfilling a trapping experience that may have been rerun mentally for years, were powerful motivators. Due to circumstances beyond our control, a whole generation of North American falconers has lost an assortment of hawk trapping and training skills. Perhaps even more poignant, they were denied the shared challenges and experiences that molded and coalesced the old guard of North American falconry.

The pursuit of game hawking in North America has taken a quantum leap since the 1960s. This truly is where U.S. and Canadian falconers have left their mark. Looking to the future, one can only imagine that grouse hawking in the lonely reaches of the West will always have an allure for the stout of heart. And what about our comrades in the Arctic wilderness known as the Alaska bush? In my estimation, anyone who pursues ptarmigan with gyrfalcons in sub-zero temperatures from a snow machine is definitely on the cutting edge. These hardy souls face not only the elements, but the likely prospect of something lethal, like a moose or brown bear, that adds an element of fear few of us "down below" face on a day-to-day basis. In the intermountain West, the widely distributed chukar partridge may afford falconers the opportunity to test their skills in the dry desert ranges. Himalayan snow partridge, huge birds that live on mountain tops in Nevada, might be worth the effort. The Rocky Mountains are home to high-elevation ptarmigan that might also provide challenging sport for trained falcons. One could envision packing in on horseback, or perhaps being helicoptered up to some remote mountain setting, to set up base camp.

This combination of mountaineering and falconry would indeed feel like hawking at the top of the world!

I see a future in which raptor populations are managed in a manner consistent with other wildlife species, based on sound scientific data. Migrant tundra peregrines will be harvested annually for falconry. Beach trapping and the use of passage tundra peregrines, significant parts of our North American sporting heritage, will be preserved. There will be no provincial constraints on the harvest of nonendangered gyrfalcons, Peale's peregrines, and tundra peregrines by American falconers, regardless of their state of residence. Falcons and other raptors will be harvested from extensive public lands in the far north and along the eastern and southern coasts. I see any state that issues permits for out-of-state hunting and fishing also offering reasonably priced (perhaps standardized) out-of-state falconry capture permits. I envision the U.S. Fish and Wildlife Service intervening on falconry's behalf; all migratory birds fall under its protection, and the agency has leverage in the millions of dollars it gives states annually for hunting and fishing programs. Finally, I see captive, self-sustaining populations of birds of prey being regulated in the same manner already established for other migratory bird species. Legal precedence, long established for the private ownership of other captive wildlife species, will be applied without prejudice.

I also see a world where the industry that begat DDT, and other deleterious pesticides, is made accountable for its environmental abuses through toxic chemical production taxes. As a primary obligation, it will be required to invent and invest in short-term, nontoxic pesticides to replace products like DDT. Funds collected from these levies will be dedicated to support international research on wildlife species (like peregrines) that serve as "environmental barometers," and provide long-term financial support to conservation organizations, like The Peregrine Fund, that deal responsibly with the negatives of our "better living through chemistry."

Two North American falconers, Tom Cade and Morlan Nelson, are internationally famous for their conservation efforts. I believe that falconers must maintain leadership roles in both local and global affairs affecting falconry and raptor conservation. Involvement and communication, essentials to a proactive political stance, will ensure that falconry's interests will be served both at home and abroad.

The new antagonists, replacing oologists and shooters, are the so-called "animal rights" and "anti-hunting" supporters. In the U.S., they are recruited from the 93 percent of the population that neither knows about, nor participates in, any form of hunting or fishing. By and large these are urbanites, people with no frame of reference by which to judge consumptive outdoor pursuits. Poll this population with the question: who is the wildlife expert in this country? and most of them might answer, Walt Disney!

Playing skillfully on emotion and ignorance, their leaders collect millions of dollars for lobbying efforts. These people saw how effectively the political process was wielded to protect birds of prey. They are now attempting to use many of the same tactics to abolish all field sports, including falconry. Constant vigilance and competent legal counsel are the best methods to combat these adversaries. For the individual falconer, membership in the national falconry association and a modest tithing for legal defense may be the best ways to safeguard our long-term hunting rights.

My conclusion, based on the events of the past twenty years, is that falconry's most powerful tool is public relations. A knowledgeable public, accepting and supporting the sport, will greatly enhance our political stance and stature. To that end, I believe that the North American Falconers Association should develop a comprehensive strategy to market falconry values. One way to do this would be through the creation of a national center, dedicated solely to the art and practice of falconry.

In my mind, I see a falconry center located on a large tract of land, perhaps in the northern plains, scientifically managed for upland game bird and waterfowl production. The center would serve three purposes. First, it would create a place for the public to see the practice of falconry. A picture may be worth a thousand words, but nothing is as meaningful, or indelible, as a firsthand experience. Falconry is something that people must see in action to fully appreciate. Second, it would create a place for falconers to congregate, share personal experiences, and further refine their sport. Lastly, it would act as a habitat demonstration area for falconers to show, by example, how quality game management in North America can proceed.

We already have the necessary management tools. Through the judicious use of areas set aside to create year-round cover, controlled burning and grazing to govern plant successional stages, low-impact farming, wetlands preservation, and water impoundments to contain ephemeral moisture, wildlife can be attracted and grown in great numbers. At the falconry center, native prairie grouse and waterfowl, the highly revered species that need our help the most, would benefit directly from falconers. A successful falconry center might also lead to the establishment of other satellite falconry demonstration areas around the country.

It has been in the self-interest of falconers to rally for other relevant causes (environmental protection, raptor management, captive breeding, etc.). As a group, we must continue to have impact in these arenas. But the time has also come for falconers to promote their own identity. Falconers can either serve or be served, act or be acted upon.

Even within the highly industrialized countries of western Europe and North America, falconry will survive in some form. It may not always include the use of peregrines or traditional game species, but the art itself will be perpetuated.

Of all field sports, falconry remains unique. According to a federal study, neither the taking of birds of prey from the wild nor the killing of game with trained raptors is shown to have any biological impact on wildlife populations. Banding studies of wild peregrine and prairie falcons show that approximately 75 percent of the immatures, birds of the year, perish before their first spring. A falcon trapped and flown through its first winter by a falconer may actually have a greater chance of surviving to maturity than a wild bird.

Falconry is as true an approximation of a nonconsumptive hunting sport as exists in the world today. In essence, falconry is a commitment to a life in service to a bird. It is a passionate relationship with a magnificent living creature, unlike ownership of an inanimate object like a firearm or fishing rod.

Falcons are not now, nor have they ever been, "bullets that fly around corners." Any person flying a falcon at game should expect no more than modest success under the conditions present throughout most of North America. By contrast, a decent wing shooter, spending the same number of hours in the field, would certainly have much to brag about and a full freezer as proof. But the essence of falconry is the sport itself. In the past two decades, the American sporting scene has undergone radical changes. Participants now judge their outdoor experiences by an index of recreational quality. An aesthetically fine day in the field without a kill may register higher than a slovenly afternoon of meat hunting. Legions of bow hunters, muzzle loaders, barbless fly fishermen, and photo buffs take to the field to enjoy wildlife and the outdoors in their own special way. Increased population pressures and urban sprawl are shrinking rural areas. Public access is restricted to the remaining parcels. Herein lies one of falconry's greatest attributes: falconers do not pepper houses and cripple livestock with shot. In addition, many semiurban areas now support large numbers of game birds in zones (city limits, parks, and industrial areas) that prohibit shooting. In some regions, these are the only sane places left to fly a trained hawk during the gun hunting season.

To me, falconry is a direct line of communication. Much of what we think, feel, and know today comes through impersonal intermediary devices such as television, radio, computers, fax machines, and telephones. As the world becomes more populated, it seems increasingly dehumanized. We satisfy our needs to participate and communicate with our surroundings in many different ways: some people raise animals, some grow things in dirt, some hunt and fish. It is, in essence, the same expression; an emotional, one-to-one linkup with the incalculable forces that surround us. These activities soothe the soul and rejuvenate the spirit, a "product" that, much to their chagrin, Madison Avenue advertising executives can't sell. For the majority of falconers, their sport is an emotional form of "urban renewal," a means to recharge their batteries, a quick reality check, a stabilizing force. It is the celebration of life.

Falconry has evolved from a practical means of putting food on the table to a highly refined art form; the falcon's wingbeats across the sky have been likened to the strokes of a painter's brush on canvas. One-of-a-kind experiences, like finding an eyrie, raising an eyas, trapping a passage falcon, or witnessing a truly spectacular flight by a falcon working in concert with man and dog, become mental pictures long remembered. In many ways, falconry is a return to basics, a vehicle for communing with nature on its level. These experiences are real. To me, falconry is the antithesis of mediocrity—a lucid rejection of the brain-numbing, mass media hype that stifles the individual's spirit and creativity. Despite scientific and technological advances, the essence of falconry for many of its participants remains mystical, religious, and deeply personal. Trained hawks are a reflection of a person's talents and aspirations. May it ever be so.

Glossary of Terms

Accipiter—the family of maneuverable woodland hawks characterized by relatively short, rounded wings, a long tail, and reddish eyes.

Anglo-Indian hood—a one-piece Indian hood to which braces are attached to facilitate opening and closing.

Arab hood—a one-piece hood, similar to a Dutch hood in appearance, that is unblocked, with an accordion back.

Aspergillosis—a fungal disease of the upper respiratory tract that often attacks northern raptors trapped in southern latitudes and desert species kept in warm, moist climates—primary symptom is excessive thirst.

Austringer—a person who flies the short-winged hawks exclusively.

Aylmeri—leather anklets attached to the raptor's legs by means of a grommet. The grommet hole allows the insertion of slitted jesses for restraining the bird or the removal of jesses when the bird is to be flown. With this system, the bird cannot become snared or tangled by its jesses if lost.

Bagged game—any game artificially released for a raptor to chase.

Bate—the action of a tethered raptor that attempts to fly.

Bal-chatri—a dome-shaped wire cage with nooses tied to the top, used primarily for trapping woodland hawks and kestrels.

Bells—small, specially made bells used for locating raptors when out of sight.
Bewit—leather thongs for fastening bells or transmitters to a raptor's leg above the jess.
Bind—to grab and hold quarry.
Block—a cylindrical, post-like perch used for perching falcons outside.
Bow net—a trap consisting of two hinged hoops and a net which may be flipped over a raptor that is attracted to bait on the ground.
Braces—leather straps which open and close a hood.
Brancher—a young short-winged hawk which has left the nest but still resides with the parents.
Break into—the act of a raptor depluming its prey and beginning to eat.
Buteo—any one of the soaring hawks with broad, rounded wings, a short tail, and yellow eyes.
Cadge—a field perch to transport falcons.
Call off—beckoning a raptor to come for food.
Carry—the vice of a raptor when it flies away with its quarry.
Cast—to grab and restrain a raptor with both hands for administering medicine, coping, etc.
Casting—the pellet disgorged by all raptors following a meal.
Cast off—to release a raptor to fly at game.
Cast of falcons—two or more falcons trained to hunt in unison.
Cere—the fleshy part of the beak above the horn.
Check—when a falcon chases unintended quarry.
Cliffer—a fledged eyas falcon remaining in the vicinity of the eyrie; the longwing equivalent of a brancher.
Coccidiosis—an intestinal malady caused by protozoan—early symptoms are blood specks in the mutes.
Cope—the trimming of overgrown beaks and talons.
Crab—fighting between two trained hawks or falcons.
Creance—a safety line used in the early stages of training.
Crop—the storage area for food below the upper esophagus.
Deck feathers—the central two tail feathers.
Dho-gazza—a mist net used for trapping raptors.

Downy—the growth stage before a young raptor has grown body feathers.
Draw the hood—to close the hood.
Dutch hood—traditionally, a three-piece hood, molded on a block shaped like a falcon's head.
Enseam—to purge a raptor of excess fat prior to the hunting season by feeding small stones (wrangle).
Enter—to start capturing a particular quarry.
Eyas—a young raptor obtained from a nest.
Eyrie—the classical name for a falcon's nest.
Falcon—a specialized hawk with dark eyes, long, narrow wings and a special notch or "tooth" in its beak for dispatching prey. Formerly the term applied only to females of the species.
Falconer—formerly, one who trained long-winged falcons exclusively; now describes anyone who trains raptors.
False point—the vice of a bird dog that points imaginary game birds.
Feak—the stropping (cleaning) of a beak after a meal.
Feathers in the blood—new feathers that are still growing.
Feed up—the satiating of a raptor's appetite, generally from a kill.
Flight out of the hood—a direct chase whereby game is sighted and the falcon is released from the fist. The traditional method used in Arab hawking and for ringing flights, with quarry such as rooks and crows.
Foot—the act of hitting or grabbing game.
Fret marks (hunger streaks)—lines visible across new feathers—thought to weaken the shaft as a result of stress or poor diet.
Frounce (pigeon canker)—a protozoan infection (trichomoniasis) of the mouth and respiratory tract that is widely transmitted by pigeons and doves. Early symptoms are yellowish "cheese" in the raptor's mouth and an unwillingness to swallow food. Today, this malady is easily controlled by drugs.
Game hawk—technically, a falcon trained to hunt from a waiting-on position.

Gerkin—a male gyrfalcon.
Gorge—to allow a raptor to eat its fill.
Goshawk—the largest accipiter or "short-winged" hawk.
Gyrfalcon—the largest falcon and the fastest in level flight.
Hack—the period of freedom allowed young falcons while they are still dependent on food provided by the falconer.
Haggard—an adult raptor.
Hard-penned (full summed)—the point at which all new feathers have grown into a young raptor and no longer have blood in the shafts; also, the completion of a molt.
Hawk chalk—a nickname for hawk droppings; also, the title of the triannual publication of the North American Falconers' Association.
Hawking bag—the falconer's kit for carrying food, the lure, assorted equipment, and game.
High—a term describing a raptor thats weight is too far above its optimum flying weight to risk flying it in the field.
Hood—a close-fitting leather hat covering the eyes used to immobilize raptors during training, handling, and transportation.
Hood block—the form in the shape of a falcon's head, upon which Dutch hoods are molded.
Hood shy—a raptor that dislikes or is afraid of the hood.
Hybrid falcon—the offspring of an interspecies cross between falcons.
Imp—the repair of broken feathers.
Imprint—a young raptor that was raised by hand and is psychologically bonded to its trainer.
Indian hood—a one-piece hood, sewn up the sides and back, with a wide, comfortable beak opening. Genuine Indian hoods must be crammed over the falcon's head to fit.
Intermewed—a falcon that has been kept through the molt.
Jesses—leather straps attached to the falcon's legs.
Keen—a state of hunger at which time a falcon is ready to fly.
Lanner—a medium-sized desert falcon from Africa and Eurasia.
Leash—a leather or synthetic thong used to tie a falcon to its perch.

Longwing—a true falcon.
Low—describes a lack of weight or physical condition.
Lure—a dummy or simulated bird body used to retrieve a falcon.
Make hawk—an experienced falcon used to educate an inexperienced falcon by example.
Make in—to approach the falcon on the ground.
Man—the process of taming a wild falcon.
Mantle—the act of a falcon covering food or a kill with its wings.
Mar hawk—a falcon or hawk ruined for hunting purposes.
Mark down—to sight the exact location of quarry.
Merlin—a small, bird-catching falcon.
Mews—the building that houses trained falcons.
Molt—the annual replacement of feathers.
Mount—when a falcon rises and circles above the falconer.
Mutes—hawk droppings.
Pandam—a circular noose trap for catching falcons.
Passage—an immature falcon trapped on migration.
Pigeon harness—a leather jacket with nooses attached, used to trap falcons.
Pitch—the height to which a falcon rises above the ground.
Plume a kill—to pluck or defeather.
Put in to cover—when quarry hides to avoid the falcon.
Put over a crop—the digestion of a crop of food.
Quarry—the game that the falcon chases.
Rangle—small, smooth stones given to falcons to purge them of fat accumulated in the crop.
Rake away—when a falcon leaves the area.
Raptor—a term used to describe all birds of prey.
Reclaim—the retraining of a falcon after the molt, or the recovery of a lost falcon.
Refuse quarry—when a falcon does not chase flushed quarry.
Ringing flight—a direct chase of quarry high into the air from the fist.
Ring perch—a circular metal perch for short-winged hawks.
Ring up to—a method of mounting whereby the falcon circles up above the falconer while gaining a pitch.

Glossary of Terms   235

Round perch—a padded cylindrical perch mounted vertically at chest height. The falcon is secured to the top of the 8-inch diameter perch at jess length.
Rouse—when a falcon shakes its feathers.
Sails—a falcon's wings.
Saker—a large desert falcon from Eurasia and Africa; the favorite bird of Arab falconers.
Screen perch—a padded, horizontal bar perch mounted chest-high off the ground. Falcons are tied to the top, permitting swivel action, but mobility is limited to the length of the jesses. A taut screen hangs below to prevent the falcon from rounding the bar. A dangerous perch if unattended.
Seel—the practice of sewing a falcon's eyelids together.
Serve game—to flush game.
Shaheen—a small desert falcon of the Middle East and Asia.
Sharp set—hungry
Shelf perch—a padded, half-circle wooden shelf, with an 8-inch radius, attached to a wall. A "screw eye" or ring is fixed below for tethering the falcon. Outdoors, the perch can be used for weathering. Indoors, it is generally mounted twelve inches above a carpeted subfloor. A safe and practical way to constrain falcons.
Shift—the evasive dodging of prey in the air.
Short-winged hawk—an accipiter hawk.
Slip—a hunting opportunity; to release the hawk after quarry.
Soaring—the effortless flying of a falcon via thermal lift.
Sock—a nylon stocking used to constrain a newly trapped falcon.
Stoop—a high-speed dive.
Strike—the hit on quarry.
Strike the hood—to open the braces to remove the hood.
Swivel—a noncorrosive figure "8" metal swivel. Jesses are attached to one ring and the leash to the other. The swivel keeps the other equipment from becoming tangled.
Take stand—when the falcon sits, often above where quarry has put in.
Telemetry—electronic tracking equipment used to retrieve lost falcons.

Throw up—a return to high altitude from the outrun of a stoop.
Tiercel—a male falcon.
Tidbit—a morsel of food given as a reward.
Tiring—a diversion for the falcon; often a tough or bony piece of meat to keep the bird occupied.
Train—the falcon's tail.
Trap—to catch a wild falcon.
Truss—to bind to quarry.
Wait-on—to circle high in the air over the falconer.
Wake—the practice of carrying a newly trapped falcon for several days nonstop. The falcon becomes exhausted and submits to training quickly.
Warbel—when a falcon hitches both wings over its back and fans the tail—a means of stretching.
Washed meat—meat strips soaked in water to remove all nutritional contents.
Weather—to perch the falcon in the open air, generally on a lawn or in an enclosure for protection.
Weathering enclosure—a fenced and covered area that allows a falcon fresh air and sunshine while providing protection from people and animals, as well as inclement weather.

Suggested Reading

Beebe, F. L. 1961. Peregrines and waterfowl. *Falconry News and Notes.* 2(3): 1–10.
——— 1992. *The Compleat Falconer.* Hancock House Publishers, Surrey, B.C. 336 pp.
Beebe, F. L. and H. M. Webster. 1964. *North American Falconry and Hunting Hawks.* Denver, CO. 315 pp.
Blaine, G. 1970. *Falconry.* Charles T. Branford Co., Newton, MA. 253 pp.
Boyd, L. 1968. Partridge hawking. *Journal of North American Falconers' Assoc.* 12: 24–25.
Browning, C. 1982. Targhee—Gamehawking with an eyas prairie. *Journal of North American Falconers' Assoc.* 21: 56–71.
Chindgren, S. 1973. The passage prairie falcon. *Utah Falconers' Assoc. Journal* 1972–73: 16–17.
Connolly, M. 1968. Duck hawking tactics. *Journal of North American Falconers' Assoc.* 7: 10–12.
——— 1969. Pond duck hawking tactics. *Hawk Chalk* 8(2): 31–36.
——— 1975. Falcons and the water syndrome. *Hawk Chalk* 14(1): 44–48.
Duecker, S. 1982. Pheasant hawking. *Journal of North American Falconers' Assoc.* 21: 102–107.
Frederick II of Hohenstaufen. 1943. *The Art of Falconry. (De Arte Venendi Cum Avibus).* Translated by Dr. Casey A. Wood

and F. Marjorie Fyfe. Stanford Univ. Press, Palo Alto, CA.
Glasier, P. 1978. Falconry and Hawking. Charles T. Branford Co., Newton, MA. 312 pp.
Gossard, T. 1970. Hawking pond and brook with the peregrine. *J. N. Amer. Falconers' Assoc.* 9: 13–21.
Guthormsen, D. W. 1973. Pigeons and falcons. *Hawk Chalk* 12(1): 39–40.
────── 1977. Mistakes learned from game hawking prairie falcons. *The Journal, California Hawking Club.* 102–107.
────── 1981. North American classics. *J. N. Amer. Falconers' Assoc.* 20: 70–75.
────── 1985. Northern prairie sharptail flights. *J. N. Amer. Falconers' Assoc.* 24: 30–38.
Haak, B. A. 1980. Hybrid falcons. *J. N. Amer. Falconers' Assoc.* 18–19: 74–83.
────── 1981. Duck hawking and big water techniques. *J. N. Amer. Falconers' Assoc.* 20: 36–41.
────── 1988. Kudos for Kudu. *J. N. Amer. Falconers' Assoc.* 27: 47–53.
Haak, B. A. and C. Merker. 1981. Tame hacking eyas falcons. *J. N. Amer. Falconers' Assoc.* 20: 12–19.
Hayes, G. 1976. So "Tahoe" hath her desires. *J. N. Amer. Falconers' Assoc.* 15: 33–36.
Haschak, A. 1983. Mr. Jaxom. *J. N. Amer. Falconers' Assoc.* 22: 50–55.
────── 1986. Snipe...the ultimate quarry? *J. N. Amer. Falconers's Assoc.* 25: 32–33.
Konkel, D. 1976. A Colorado prairie duck hawk. *J. N. Amer. Falconers' Assoc.* 15: 28–29.
Mavrogordato, J. G. 1960. *A Hawk for the Bush.* Charles T. Branford Co., Newton, MA. 144 pp.
────── 1966. *A Falcon in the Field.* Knightly Vernon Ltd., London. 123 pp.
Michell, E. B. 1964. *The Art and Practice of Falconry.* Charles T. Branford Co., Newton, MA. 291 pp.
Moritsch, M. Q. 1983. Photographic guide for aging nestling prairie falcons. *USDI, Bureau of Land Management. Snake*

River Birds of Prey Project. Boise, ID. 8 pp.

Pineo, D. 1982. Tales from the Palouse. *J. N. Amer. Falconers' Assoc.* 21: 82–89.

Rafuse, B. and D. Guthormsen. 1975. Ultimate game hawk: the eyas prairie falcon. *J. N. Amer. Falconers' Assoc.* 14: 6–10.

Robertson, T. 1976. Training the passage prairie falcon. *California Hawking* 6(1): 29–31.

Rogers, R. 1982. Lesser prairie chickens on the Llano Estacado. *J. N. Amer. Falconers' Assoc.* 21: 6–13.

Schwartz, C. H. and M. Browne. 1978. Raising imprint merlins. *Hawk Chalk* 17(1): 38–46.

Sherrod, S. K., W. R. Heinrich, W. A. Burnham, J. H. Barclay and T. J. Cade. 1981. Hacking: a method for releasing peregrine falcons and other birds of prey. *The Peregrine Fund, Inc.,* Ithaca, NY. 61 pp.

Stevens, R. 1978. *Observations on Modern Falconry.* Falconiforme Press, Saskatoon, Sask. 112 pp.

Taggart, J. P., III. 1975. Game hawking the Hungarian partridge. *J. N. Amer. Falconers' Assoc.* 14: 14.

Turner, R. and A. Haslen. 1991. *Gamehawk.* Gallery Press, Lavenham, England. 140 pp.

Walker, W., II. 1968. Quail hawking in Colorado. *J. N. Amer. Falconers' Assoc.* 12: 22–23.

Weaver, J. D. and T. J. Cade (eds.). 1983. Falcon propagation: A manual on captive breeding. *The Peregrine Fund, Inc.,* Ithaca, NY. 93 pp.

Webster, H. A. and J. H. Enderson. 1988. *Game Hawking...At Its Very Best.* Windsong Press, Denver, CO. 316 pp.

Widener, P., Jr. 1975. Hawking the sharp-tailed grouse. *J. N. Amer. Falconers' Assoc.* 14: 11–13.

Woodford, M. 1960. *A Manual of Falconry.* Charles T. Branford Co., Newton, MA. 192 pp.

Younghans, M. 1969. Duck hawking with an eyas Peale's falcon. *J. N. Amer. Falconers' Assoc.* 14: 17–19.

NATURE BOOKS FROM HANCOCK HOUSE

ISBN 0-88839-253-2

ISBN 0-88839-306-7

ISBN 0-88839-217-6

ISBN 0-88839-978-2

ISBN 0-88839-311-3

ISBN 0-88839-280-X

ISBN 0-88839-310-5

Order from

HANCOCK WILDLIFE RESEARCH CENTER

1431 Harrison Avenue
Blaine, WA U.S.A. 98231
Phone: (206) 354-6953
Fax: (604) 538-2262